If I Had a Face Like Yours

If I Had a Face Like Yours

Glyn Barrett

New Wine Press

New Wine Ministries
PO Box 17
Chichester
West Sussex
United Kingdom
PO19 2AW

ISBN 1-903725-83-6

Typeset by CRB Associates, Reepham, Norfolk
Cover design by CCD, www.ccdgroup.co.uk
Printed in Malta

Contents

Dedication

To Georgia and Jaedon – the greatest kids in the world. Great faces, great personalities, great adventure, awesome future. I love you heaps!

Acknowledgements

To Sophia, thanks for your love, support and all the hours you invest and sacrifice into seeing a radical reinvention of church in this nation.

To Mum and Sian, thanks for helping me to formulate much of the thinking contained within this book.

Dave and Jenny, you have been great pastors for the last decade. Thanks for your inspiration and vision.

Hope City Church, you are great people. Thanks for being the guinea pigs for much of the information in this book.

Hazel, Gill and Sophia, thanks for your help in editing this book. One of you is English, one Irish and the other Australian – who knows if it will make sense!

Stuart, I appreciate your friendship and long phone calls. You are building a great church!

Nick and Caroline, Lindsey, Naomi, Matt (AKA Chalky) and Lindsay, Chris and Gosia, Mark and Em, Andy and Karen, Elaine, Miriam, Deanna, Rob and Rach – you guys make life and work fun, just like it should be!

Miriam and Gemma, thanks for typing and listening and typing and listening!

Paul and Rachel in Youth Alive UK, you are legends who are fast creating a legend!

9

Derek, Michael, Mark and Andy, Audacious shouldn't be this much fun!

Jesus, there is a generation living to hear people say to them, "I don't know what you are smoking, drinking, chewing or injecting, but I gotta get me some of that!" Living for You is flippin' brilliant!

Someone once said,

"If quitters never win and
winners never quit!,
then who the heck said,
'Quit while you're ahead'?"

Chapter 1

The part you just HAVE to read

I don't mean to be rude (well, perhaps just a little), but what is going on with people's faces? Here is a poem by me!

"Faces"

Some are long,
some are fat;
some are rosy and others suit a hat.

Some are HUGE,
some are small;
some are tanned and others tall.

Some have two eyebrows
others one;
some look like they need some fun.

Where one is happy,
the other sad;
one is good, the other ... well ... bad.

The point is simple,
the facts are clear;
your face shows me what you hold most dear.

Whatever you believe,
I'll know it's true,
it will stick to your face just like glue!

In case you were wondering, this book does not advocate plastic surgery, face-lifts or botox injections. All those are well and good, if that's what you need. *If I Had a Face Like Yours* is a challenge to everyone who may feel like things are a little bit samey, mediocre, tedious or boring.

For those of you who have a relationship with God, this book is a wake up call! It is shouting,

• If you believe in God, at least look like you do. The sooner you realise that "boring" and "God" don't go together, the sooner you can enjoy life to the absolute max.

For church leaders and youth pastors or leaders, the book is shouting,

• Lighten up. Christianity is meant to be fun and church should be the most exciting place to be.

If you don't know the God of the Bible, get ready for the shock of your life. This book is shouting,

• God is not who you think He is!

Someone once said to me, "Why should I go to church? I have enough problems of my own." Surely Jesus didn't die on the cross to give us a boring life? What a shame that this friend of mine sees church as anything but full of Good

News! What a shame that God is given such a bad name by those who say they follow Him.

I feel like saying to some Christians, *"If I had a face like yours, I would be an undertaker!"*[1]

The oxymoron that is "boring church"

An oxymoron is defined in the dictionary as "a figure of speech in which apparently contradictory terms appear in conjunction". Confused? Me too. Here are some examples to help you understand what an oxymoron is:

- Beautiful feet; false fact; unbelievably true; sincere liar; perfectly wrong; she's the man; meteoric rise; exact opposite; bus timetable; worst enemy; lady driver (sorry girls); male intelligence (sorry guys)

Similarly the terms "boring church", "irrelevant Christian" and "tedious sermons" are all oxymorons. They should simply not be! Later in the book you will discover why both church and life should be phenomenal and how it can be so.

Wise words from Mark Twain

Mark Twain once famously said, "Tradition is not wearing your grandfather's hat; it's buying a new one like he did."[2]

If I were to wear my granddad's hat down the main street in the city where I live, people would look at me and think one of two things: either,

1. I am irrelevant and out of touch, or
2. I am a poor university student, forced to buy second-hand clothes! (to be read slightly tongue in cheek).

The Church is the only "club" that exists for non-members. As a member of a gym I have exclusive rights: free towel, free shampoo and shower gel,[3] the use of the pool and equipment is unlimited and the member's lounge is available for me to use at my leisure. The Church on the other hand exists not primarily for those who are in the "club", but for those who are yet to know about the "Good News" of Jesus and "join up".

All too often, when people attend a church service, they are confronted with "granddad's hat". A church that in style and liturgy represents something that is somewhat antiquated (meaning "old-fashioned") and irrelevant to the needs of the modern-day businessman, single parent, tradesman, job seeker or student. The potential new "member" is left feeling that God, therefore, must be old-fashioned because that is the way He is presented. (From a youth perspective, old-fashioned and boring mean the same thing.)

Mark Twain got it right! We shouldn't do things the way we have always done them in church because tradition is not doing the same thing again and again – it is the right to invent a new way of doing things. Tradition does not mean observing old or best practice, it really means creating new practice.[4] In other words, buying a NEW HAT like granddad did!

The modern-day follower of Christ is someone who truly understands that our heritage is not our destiny. We thank God for everything that has been, but we realise that if our future is indistinguishable from our past, then we have no future.

If we followed the wise words of Mark Twain, God would probably not have the bad image problem that He currently has.

The barber shop

For years I went to a barber shop to get my hair cut. (I used to call him "the butchers" because of what he would do to my hair. To say that it was hacked was a serious understatement.) My barber was what you could call a "man's man". On a Friday night he would go out with the lads and drink up to twelve pints of beer (after all, he had to pace himself). On Saturday night he would drink up to sixteen pints of beer and then on a Sunday night, anywhere over sixteen pints was classified as a great night out.

The greatest wisdom relating to that particular barber shop was ensuring you never went for a haircut on a Saturday or a Monday morning. The combination of a hangover and sharp scissors was never good, as the increasing rate of one-eared people in the community can testify.

After several years of getting my hair cut, my barber one day said, "Glyn, why do you never look depressed, never complain or ever look miserable?" So I told him once again about the difference that a relationship with God makes in a person's life. After several minutes he asked, "How can I know that God is really there?" I replied by telling him to pray and ask God to show Himself to him, to which he agreed.

Three weeks later I went back to the barber's. As I opened the door I noticed that there were seven people waiting to have their hair cut. There were two men already having their hair done by the two barbers in the shop, which meant there were nine men, plus me. I estimated that if each barber took twenty minutes per head (or ear, depending on the day), this was going to be a long wait! Just as I was about to leave (I wasn't waiting), my barber spotted me and shouted, "Glyn, I did it!" "What did you do?" I asked. He shouted again, "I did it!" "Yeah, but what did you do?" I repeated "I did it!" he said again. "But what did you do?" I shot back (I hadn't forgotten, I was just baiting him!). "I did it!" he insisted. This time everyone in the shop shouted, "But what did you do?" He replied, "I prayed to God!" The bottom jaw of everyone dropped. I asked him for the last time, "What happened?" He answered, "I had a dream and I saw God! Tell me more about Him!" So I did. I leant against the door of the shop. No one could leave and no one was coming in. This was CHURCH!

That whole opportunity came about because the barber noticed something about the way I did life and something about my face showed that I really lived what I believed. The Gospel wasn't just good news in theory. It wasn't just rhetoric in a book called the Bible. It was truth and it affected the way I lived.

This book is designed to help you do that. It has been crafted to help you change your face so that when people look at you, their natural reaction is, *"I don't know what you're smoking, drinking, chewing or injecting, but I gotta get me some of that!"*

That is effectively what my barber said to me! Maybe not in so many words, but something about the way I lived life for God showed on my face and it was something that he really wanted.

St Francis of Assisi[5] said, "Share the Gospel and use words if you must!" In other words, your face and your lifestyle should shout to the world *"This God stuff is GOOD NEWS!"* If I may be so bold to ask ... does it? Does your face, your lifestyle, your Christianity, your church reflect a God who is incredible, amazing, awe-inspiring, funny, adventurous, life-giving and brilliant?

This book is written to youth, young adults, parents, pastors and leaders. If we ever meet, I hope I don't think "If I had a face like yours, I'd be an undertaker",[6] but rather, "I wish I had a face like yours!"

Coming up:
"Baked beans and social problems!"

Notes

1. I am continually amazed that you often have to walk through a graveyard in order to get into many churches. What a nightmare for advertising people. Usually you make the outside of a building attractive in order to invite people in. Not churches. We put dead people outside and say to everyone, "Come in and have some fun!" – Not likely!

2. Mark Twain was an American humorist, novelist, writer and lecturer.

3. Technically, I know it's not free. I pay £37.00 per month to be in this gym!

4. I believe that the message of Jesus has not changed. However, our style of presentation has to be relevant for today, presenting God as He is – totally relevant to everyone.

5. St Francis of Assisi is a famous Catholic saint. Born 1182 AD in Assisi (Italy) and died 1228 AD.

6. **Author's note**: In case you wonder what I look like, let me give you a brief description. People have said I have a touch of Brad Pitt with a hint of George Clooney in looks. I have the torso (upper body) of Mr Incredible and the legs of a champion body-builder. Do you believe me? Check out the back cover!

Someone once said,

> "We could all take a lesson
> from the weather. It pays no
> attention to criticism!"

Chapter 2

The part you REALLY HAVE to read!

There is a book in the Bible called Ephesians. To say that it is "quality" is a massive understatement and simply does not begin to describe how brilliant it is. It is like comparing...

- **PSPs to the old pinball parlours** that had one or two rickety table football games and PAC MAN with a fuzzy screen (how many of you remember Pac Man? ... I see those two hands!)
- **OR – iPODs to portable CD players** that jump when you move. What a shambles they were (although they did help us to get to the stage where iPODs and the subsequent generations of them could rule the world!)
- OR – the latest **boy band with U2** – it is just wrong!

Ephesians is the PSP of books. It is the iPOD of storytelling and the U2 of life-changing impact! The book of Ephesians is actually a letter that a guy called Paul wrote to the people who were going to church in the city of Ephesus, in Turkey. At the time of writing, Ephesus had a population of anywhere up to 500,000 people. When Paul was writing he was under house arrest in Rome (that is another wicked story for another time). The etiquette of letter writing is fourfold.

1. Have a purpose for writing

You must have written a letter before. Usually you write it
for a reason. It may be because you are a university student
and need money from your parents because you have been
wearing granddad's hat and eating baked beans for six
months, both of which are ultimately creating a problem in
your social life because,

(a) You look like a very old man
(b) You smell

2. Start the letter with an appropriate line which states who you are writing to

It would be completely pointless if you wanted money from
your mum, but started the letter with "Dear Auntie Gertrude".
Mum would be confused, annoyed and disappointed and you
probably wouldn't get your money, leaving you with a social
problem that is both antiquated and smelly.

3. Get to the point and make it clear

What can be worse than watching a movie that takes nine
years to watch (yet another epic), when really they could

have scripted and edited it to take only an hour and a half of your time rather than nine years? Similarly, there is nothing worse than reading a letter that takes ninety-seven years to read (slight exaggeration), when one or two paragraphs could have clearly stated what needed to be said. Waffle is a killer to anything that is written with the intention of making an impact. Waffle is defined in the dictionary as, "speaking or writing vaguely, pointlessly and at considerable length". In other words, going on and on and on about stuff that no one really cares about, like an old man's hat and baked beans and letter writing to mum and ... and .... and ... and (in case you haven't figured it out yet, I have just waffled for the last paragraph or so! Annoying isn't it?) GET TO THE POINT!

4. Can't think of a fourth point!

So Paul writes a letter to the church in Ephesus because:

1. He has a purpose to write;
2. He knows who he is writing to;
3. He has a clear point to make;
4. Can't think of a fourth reason.

Paul's purpose, people and point

As Paul sat and thought about the people in Ephesus he began to realise there were huge problems with the way the people practised their Christian faith (sound familiar?)

Ephesus was a city centred on the goddess Diana or Ephesia Artemis (see Acts 19:28 and read about the riot Paul causes in Ephesus). She was the goddess of the underworld and was inextricably (Nah, I don't know what it means either) linked with the powers and magic of the underworld.

As a child living in Ephesus you would always have been able to see the temple to the goddess situated in the valley. As a student in school your teachers would have been magicians and astrologers. Every morning you would have said incantations to scare away evil spirits and you also would have worn lucky charms around your neck to scare away demons.

The priests who worked in the temple had the evil ability to curse people and you would have known people who died from demonic curses from these evil priests. At the age of twelve you would have had to go to the temple to become a prostitute where men and women would have sex with you in order to worship the goddess. While serving in the temple you would have been responsible for killing newborn babies as a form of worship to Ephesia Artemis.

Ephesus was literally like living in Hell – and you think you have problems! Imagine how a lifestyle like that would affect you. Imagine the fear, worry, regret and pain you would carry around with you every day – horrible!

Paul writes the letter to the Ephesians (Paul's people – he knows who he is writing to) because he is aware that although many people have become Christians (followers of Jesus Christ), they still also have hurt and pain as well as a fear that Diana was really the most powerful of gods. Many of the Christians were starting to wear their lucky charms again and others were saying incantations and looking over their shoulder for fear of evil powers. Paul writes to get things straight! (Paul's purpose and point). He realises that Jesus Christ did not die on the cross for a type of Christianity that lives under the fear of other things. He realises that Christians are destined to be "the head and not the tail" (see Deuteronomy 28:13) AND SO HE WRITES!

Now that you understand the Bible bit, it's time to have your face challenged by the "Ephesian story".

Coming up:

FLUMMOXED!

Someone once said,

"If walking is so good for you,
why does my postman look like
Jabba the Hut?"

Face-lift #1

If I had a face like yours, I would...

...remember that KFC sells chicken

A few years ago my wife and I joined thousands of others in enjoying a concert with one of our favourite bands. They were loud, aggressive and very good. As the concert finished I noticed the tell-tale signs of hunger: my stomach was making more noise than the band!

As we walked out of the concert arena I asked Sophia if she was hungry, to which she replied, "I am so hungry I could eat the toenail off a low-flying duck" (actually, that was my statement to her – my wife is far more graceful). She agreed that she was indeed a bit peckish and when I suggested KFC, her eyes lit up with an expression that clearly said, "I am glad I married you; you are wise and handsome beyond compare."

The concert was in Manchester (UK) and knowing the city well, I knew that there would be no restaurant open for dining at that time of night (if there had been, it would have been robbed). So we drove to the nearest KFC and joined the waiting line of eight cars for the drive-thru experience.

The concept of "fast food" is a fundamental philosophy which establishments such as McDonalds and KFC live by. It is fast food because,

1. It is cooked quickly
2. It is unhealthy (please don't sue me)
3. It is really tasty

And most importantly ...

4. It is fast! In other words you don't have to wait long. You order it, get it, eat it and leave all within the space of two and a half seconds!

On that particular night, all I wanted was a bucket of chicken. Ten pieces – eight for me and two for my wife (she usually eats squirrel portions). During the twenty-minute wait in the drive thru, I had been thinking, drooling and salivating over the prospect of eating some chicken.

I need to ask you (the reader) a simple question here. "What does KFC stand for?" Is it,

(a) Kentucky Fried Chum?
(b) Kentucky Fried Chris?
(c) Kentucky Fried Christmas? Or,
(d) Kentucky Fried Chicken?

If you answered (a), (b) or (c), you would be very wrong and you seriously need to get out more. If you answered (d) however, you would be absolutely right.

Ok, back to the story. It is 11:45pm, Manchester city centre. I arrive at the window and the lady says, "Welcome to KFC. Sorry for your wait, may I take your order please?" "Yes," I reply, "Can I have a ten-piece bucket of chicken please?" Imagine my horror when she replies, "I'm sorry, we have no chicken!"

I was **flummoxed!** [1] NO CHICKEN? That's like Paris without French, Manchester United without fans (I wish), tea without milk, or worse still, supper without curry!

My wife turned to me at the drive thru and said, "How ironic, the very reason KFC exists and it doesn't have the goods!" We laughed and then I thought about the Church. The very reason the Church exists is Jesus. The Church is not simply about singing songs, listening to sermons, having great youth programmes and making friends. It is about the person, Jesus Christ. Sometimes you could think that the Church has forgotten that. Somehow we get so focused on the stuff of church (singing, programmes, numbers etc.) that we forget that it is all about Jesus Christ.

One preacher famously said, "If you take CHRIST out of the word CHRISTIAN, then you are left with IAN. Ian is a nice guy, but he won't help you much!" (If your name is Ian, no offence intended. I am sure you are a nice guy.)

One of the ways that Paul helps the people in Ephesus to get over their past i.e. superstitions, weariness, tiredness and depression, is to remind the Christians that their life is now centred around Jesus Christ. All too often people who call themselves Christians, the very people who are meant to be "like Christ" walk around with a face that is sombre and depressed. In other words, the very reason Christianity exists is Jesus, and when it comes down to the crucial moment many just don't have the goods – and society says, "I don't want to be a Christian, church is boring and Christians look depressed!" In other words, you have the face of an undertaker!

Paul reminds the Ephesians over and over that their life is now about Jesus. Thirty-six times Paul says, you are "in Christ", "in God", "in Jesus" etc. The effects of knowing this are amazing!

Your culture determines your face!

In Ephesians 1:1 Paul starts the letter by identifying who he is writing to. He says,

> *"Paul, an apostle of Christ Jesus by the will of God, to the saints **in Ephesus**, the faithful **in Christ Jesus**."* (emphasis added)

In making this statement, Paul is identifying a powerful truth. He is essentially telling the people that they have two homes! Their first home is in Ephesus. They were born and raised there, they went to school there, their parents and family live there and they served in the temple there. But their second home is "in Christ Jesus". Effectively, they have now moved homes. Let me explain why this is so powerful.

Every home has a certain way of doing things. Sophia's parents are from Chile (no, they are not cold. It is a country in South America). Sophia was born in Sydney, but raised in an innately South American home. My parents are from Wales (no, they are not swimmers. It is a country in Great Britain!) Because our parents are from different countries we both had completely different upbringings; we had different ways of doing things. Let me list some:

▶ *Christmas tradition:*
- *Sophia's family*: opened presents on Christmas Eve and then watched the sun rise on Christmas day on the beach, followed by a BBQ.
- *My family*: opened presents AFTER going to church on Christmas morning and then AFTER Christmas lunch.

▶ *Toilet tradition:*
- *Sophia's family*: Toilet seats down.
- *My family*: Toilet seats were allowed to be up.

▶ *Dinner tradition:*
- *Sophia's family*: Everyone would raise their voice at the dinner table as they debated world issues.
- *My family*: Meat and three veg with calm conversation.

The point is that our families had very different ways of doing even the most simple of things. Our homes determined our culture.[2]

When Paul writes to the Ephesians, he is saying that the Christians are "Ephesian" because they were born and raised there. But when they became Christians they were given a new home "in Jesus Christ". In the same way that the culture of Ephesus determined that everyone should be fearful of Ephesia Artemis, now, because they have a new home in Jesus, there is a new way of life to be lived!

Paul says it thirty six times: you are *"in Christ"*, *"in God"*, *"in Him"* etc. He is making the point that these people now have a new way of doing life.

- As an Ephesian you would live with fear. As a Christian you can live with peace (John 14:27).

- As an Ephesian you would say incantations to ward off evil spirits. As a Christian you can praise God because He is your protection (Psalm 121).
- As an Ephesian you would live with regret. As a Christian you can live with the knowledge that God has forgiven you of past mistakes (Romans 3:23–24).
- As an Ephesian you would worry about everything. As a Christian you can live without worry (Matthew 6:25).
- As an Ephesian you would believe that "Ephesia Artemis" was the greatest being of all time. As a Christian you can know that Jesus Christ is all powerful (Ephesians 1:20).

Imagine you are there!

- You live in a city of approximately 500,000 people
- The city is dominated by the temple built for the goddess Diana or Ephesia Artemis – the goddess of the underworld, linked with power and magic
- Your teachers are astrologers and magicians
- You wear lucky charms to scare off evil spirits
- You say incantations to scare away demons
- You have watched people die from demonic curses
- You have been a prostitute (or will be if you are not yet old enough)
- You have sacrificed babies on altars in the temple whilst serving as a prostitute.

You are working on the market in Ephesus when someone taps you on the shoulder and says, "A letter has just arrived for the church from Paul." You ask when the letter will be read to which your friend replies, "Tonight, in the house of Felix." (I dunno who Felix is, but it sounds like an old-fashioned Roman name.)

Later you arrive at Felix's house. The building is crammed with people who are eager to hear what Paul has written.

The "reader" stands and begins:

> *"Paul, an apostle of Christ Jesus, by the will of God, to the saints in Ephesus, the faithful in Christ Jesus. Grace and peace to you from God our Father and the Lord Jesus Christ."*
> (Ephesians 1:1–2)

You don't pick up on anything straight away, but you feel as giddy as a hippo in a bath of baked beans. The initial words of Paul are received with applause, the reader continues...

> *"I pray also that the eyes of your heart may be enlightened in order that you may know the hope to which he has called you, the riches of his glorious inheritance in the saints, and his incomparably great power for us who believe. That power is like the working of his mighty strength, which he exerted in Christ when he raised him from the dead and seated him at his right hand in the heavenly realms, far above all rule and authority, power and dominion, and every title that can be given, not only in the present age but also in the one to come. And God placed all things under his feet and appointed him to be head over everything..."*
> (Ephesians 1:18–22)

The crowd gasps and one bewildered lady raises her hand and says, "I don't understand. I always thought that Diana was the greatest being ever. Is Paul saying that Jesus is the greatest ever and that Diana is under His feet?" A silence descends and the reader says, "Yeah..."

The reader continues,

> *"And God raised us up with Christ and seated us with him in the heavenly realms in Christ Jesus."*
>
> (Ephesians 2:6)

Your friend raises his hand and asks the question that everybody else is dying to ask, "Hang on, Paul is saying that not only is Jesus seated above everything, but now he is saying that we are too! Does that mean that Diana and all her powers are under our feet too? Does that mean we don't have to fear her power and magic any more?" The stunned reader says, "Yeah ... I think so!"

The crowded room begins to fill with the kind of laugh that you laugh when you are not quite sure what to do. The reader continues to read...

> *"Now to him who is able to do immeasurably more than all we ask or imagine, according to his power that is at work within us..."* (Ephesians 3:20)

One single mum raises her hand and says, "My daughter Lydia is ten years old. Next year she has to go to the temple to endure her years as a prostitute. Only in my wildest dreams can I IMAGINE that she doesn't have to go through that. Are you saying that she may not have to go to the temple after all?"

The reader repeats Paul's words, *"Now to him who is able to do immeasurably **more than all we ask or imagine**, according to his power that is at work within us ... Yeah..."*

I think the room would have gone ballistic. The young mum would have hugged her daughter and cried. Others would have cried. You probably would have cried too as you thought to yourself two things:

1. Wow, what a God!
2. Mental note to self: "Write this in the diary!"

Finishing the face-lift!

KFC is all about chicken! Christianity is all about Jesus Christ. He is the centre of attention; He is the main attraction; He is all-powerful; He is the author of salvation; He is THE MAN! He is THE legend. The book of Colossians puts it this way:

> *"He is the image of the invisible God, the firstborn over all creation. For by him all things were created: things in heaven and on earth, visible and invisible, whether thrones or powers or rulers or authorities; all things were created by him and for him. He is before all things, and in him all things hold together."* (Colossians 1:15–17)

What a legend.

So whatever you have become convinced that Christianity is all about, remember again that it is all about JESUS! You can't do church and forget about having a relationship with Jesus. You can't be a Christian and forget it is about Jesus. Maybe the reason you have got bored over the years is because you have forgotten that it is all about Jesus and He is MASSIVE!

Your friendship with Jesus is the key to your face showing that the Gospel is Good News. So, next time you get down in the mouth about something, next time you feel depressed or feel like doing something stupid, remember that KFC sells chicken and Christianity is all about THE ONE AND ONLY, JESUS.

Coming up:
Diary of a nightmare!

Notes _____

1. Flummoxed! What a great word meaning "to confuse someone so much that they do not know what to do!" Fantastic! Your homework for today is to slip the word flummoxed into casual conversation with friends, parents and teachers! They will be flummoxed over your knowledge of the English language!
2. Culture is best defined as "a way of life".

Making it real for you!

1. Christianity is about Jesus. List three ways you may have become distracted from that fact.

   (a) ....

   (b) ....

   (c) ....

2. Think about your best friend. Name three major cultural differences between him/her and you.

   (a) ....

   (b) ....

   (c) ....

3. How will remembering that Jesus is the main thing help your face so that people will say, *"I don't know what you are smoking, drinking, chewing or injecting, but I want me some of that!"*?

   ....
   ....
   ....
   ....
   ....
   ....
   ....
   ....

Someone once said,

"Jesus said the truth will set you free. If that is true, why is it that every time I tell the truth I get sent to my room?"

Face-lift #2

If I had a face like yours, I would...

...remember that living for Jesus is flippin' brilliant

So what's all the fuss about Jesus? He is someone who lived about 2,000 years ago and yet people sing about Him, jump for Him, give money because of Him, live for Him, put stickers that look remarkably like fish on cars because of Him AND build buildings because of Him. What's all the fuss about Jesus? This Jesus stuff is definitely more than just a fad. The dictionary defines a fad as:

• An intense and widely shared enthusiasm for something, especially one that is short-lived, a craze.

I hope Manchester United football club are a fad, although I fear the worst on that one. "Jesus following" is much more than a fad! If it was simply a fad, then it would have been forgotten about a long time ago. Before I explain why living for Jesus is flippin' brilliant, here's a story about a nightmare time I once had trying to tell a bunch of teenagers about Jesus.

The challenge of preaching

Preaching is simply just telling people about Jesus. It usually involves various participants:

1. The speaker
2. The listener
3. The person bored of listening
4. The person passionate about what you are saying
5. The person desperately trying not to fall asleep because although the preacher may be interesting, the after-effects of staying up to watch "Match of the Day" highlights last night are really kicking in!

I have been in third world nations, developing nations and super-power nations. I have been with the rich, the poor and every variety of skin colour on the planet. Pick an age and I have had the awesome opportunity of preaching to them. The majority of the messages that I have preached have been to teenagers, students and young adults. I have noticed that adults are generally a far politer audience. If an adult thinks a sermon is boring, they will sit politely and nod in all the right places (while inwardly they may be cursing the day you were born), but at least they stay seated. On the other hand, THE TEENAGER, if bored, will let you know they are bored by . . .

- Talking
- Sleeping
- Making noises from various orifices
- Passing notes

- Walking out
- And the most annoying of all – unwrapping noisy sweet wrappers

Speaking to teenagers about the Gospel (preaching) can be challenging because the starting point for a teenager's understanding of God is that they think God is dead, irrelevant, or worst of all, really old!

Diary of a nightmare!

I first learned the challenge of speaking to teenagers in 1994. I was living in Sydney and I was asked to speak at a Hip Hop concert. There were eight hundred 14–19-year-olds packed into a community hall and as they were not from a church background, they had no concept of God beyond that He is dead, irrelevant, or worst of all, really old! Most of them had never heard of Jesus Christ. They just thought it was a great thing to shout whenever they stubbed their toe, blew up a dog or got stung by a bee.

The organiser of the event thought it would be great if somebody could share the Gospel so people could hear about Jesus. I was given the job of telling these drug-addicted, middle-class, party-loving, sex-crazed teens about Jesus.

It happened like this ...

> *9:45pm:* Arrive early enough to meet all the teenagers who would give me a really warm welcome and comment on what a brilliant preacher I am.

9:47: Discover the event organiser forgot to arrange
stewards. Take tickets at the door after hurriedly setting
up a table and chair at the entrance.

9:48: Break up the first fight of the night.

9:48.30: Smell a strange substance (marijuana).
Too scared to do anything about it.

9:50: Summoned to the bathroom to discover the
mirror smashed, water all over the floor and graffiti on
the doors and walls (secretly glad I am not organising
the event – imagine the bill at the end of this one).

9:58: Still taking tickets at the door.

9:59: See a boy and a girl in the corner doing stuff they
shouldn't be doing in a public place. Think about
breaking it up – too scared!

10:03: Music starts. Loud! Notice that the DJ has an
interesting hairstyle. (Mental note: make a comment
about the DJ's hair during preach – might get a laugh.)

10:03–1:00am: Wait, feeling nervous and sick.

1:00am: Get the nod – and get thrown out onto the
stage!

Picture the scene: eight hundred teenagers have been
dancing rhythmically for three hours whilst consuming
alcohol, drugs and each other. The Hip Hop band that
everybody had come to hear is waiting to perform.
The crowd are geared-up, drugged-up, boozed-up and
sexed-up when all of a sudden the music stops and I am
thrown onto the stage. The teenagers have no idea what
to expect. We exchange looks for what seems like hours.

1:00.30: I say "G'day" and two hundred people respond
with words too inappropriate to print. Remembering the
DJ's hair, I make a comment. People laugh. They think

this is a stand-up comedy routine so they begin to relax. I am tense – they are like hungry wolves looking for some prey to devour. I am the lamb led to the slaughter.

1:01: I mention the name "Jesus" for the first time and there is a riot!

I felt ALONE! Four hundred people charged the stage throwing anything they could at me: coke bottles, cigarette lighters, shoes, cigarette packets, etc. I was trying to think about what to say, but the volume was so loud I couldn't think. The more the teenagers screamed the more the DJ turned up the PA system. The noise was incredible. While four hundred people were screaming and shouting at me, another four hundred were sitting around the edges trying to listen. I spoke for four minutes!

1:04.30: I get off the stage, a nervous wreck! That was a scary experience.

1:05: The band come on stage and sing their title track: "Is that your face or did your neck throw up?" Eight hundred teenagers start to dance. I couldn't help but notice the irony: there was I, trying to tell them they were awesome and yet they preferred to sing "Is this my face or did my neck throw up?"

A few years ago I was at a big youth event in Coventry (UK). I was asked to preach on "What's all the fuss about Jesus?" The Sydney horror event taught me several lessons, the overriding one being, "if the Gospel doesn't work for teenagers then it doesn't work". If a sixteen-year-old who has seen his mum and dad get divorced and his older brother overdose on drugs can't make sense of the Gospel, then what's the point of it? It has to be relatable. It has to work.

I've spent over a decade preaching to teenagers and my answer to them, when they ask me the WHY question about Jesus, is simply:

- LIVING FOR JESUS IS FLIPPIN' BRILLIANT!

There are three reasons why living for Jesus is flippin' brilliant and why knowing this should change your face.

1. Jesus is the local

In 1996 Sophia and I moved from Sydney to run the youth ministry in Hope City Church in Sheffield (UK). We soon became aware that when teenagers go to school or college on a Monday morning, their mates boast about all the bottles of cider they consumed on Friday, while the church kids timidly whispered, "Oh yeah, I went to church."

We wanted to re-invent it so that when the church teenagers went to school on Monday they would brag about the weekend. I wanted them to say to their mates who got drunk, "That's nothing compared to what I've been doing! At church we..." and then the youth would rattle off all the non-cheesy, non-geeky, non-star-trekky things that the awesome youth ministry called "Extreme" had been doing.

In other words, we wanted to give the youth something that was so great they would look back in years to come and say "Youth was awesome!" We wanted the greatest times in their lives to be linked to Jesus.

We did crazy things like...

- Giving two older youth £1 and seeing how far they could travel by the end of the youth service or by Sunday.
- Giving the youth £5 each, teaching them the principles of making money, then asking them to make the £5 grow during the week. We made thousands of pounds!
- International day trips (I'll tell you more in a minute).

We did simple things like...

- Playing British bulldog in the "black" (which also involved visiting the accident and emergency ward).
- Camping in centuries-old barns.
- Organising twelve-hour parties and heaps of other things.

It was awesome and the youth LOVED it!

One of the craziest ideas was to visit another nation for a day. We visited various cities and towns in France, including Paris and some of the seaside towns. There are two ways in which you can see Paris:

1. Go to a local travel agent and book a tour where you'll get an English-speaking British tour guide who'll travel with you and show you the sights of Paris. That's usually good. You will see the Arc De Triomphe, The Eiffel Tower, The Louvre, Notre Dame Cathedral (incidentally, the Hunchback is not there – I looked for him).

2. Find a genuine Parisian (that's a person from Paris) and say, "Will you show me your city?" That Frenchman will not only show you the common tourist sights of Paris, but he'll also show you the back streets and bits of Paris that others miss out on. You'll come back from that trip saying, "That was brilliant!" Why? Because you got a local to take you around.

The Bible says that,

- When the world was created, Jesus was there (John 1:1).
- When life was created, Jesus created life (Genesis 1).

If you want to get the best out of life, then you have to understand that Jesus is the local. He is the Frenchman who is proud of Paris. He is the Englishman who is proud of London; He is the Aussie who loves Sydney.

If you want the best relationships, friendships, finances, marriages, then instead of turning to the stars in the morning papers or Saturday morning TV, talk to Jesus. Jesus created life so He can show you how to get the best out of life.

Jesus is fantastic! The Bible says,

> *"In all your ways acknowledge him* [God],
> *and he will make your paths straight."*
>
> (Proverbs 3:6)

One of the reasons why our lives end up in a mess is because we don't go to Jesus. If we go to Him, He will make our paths straight. In other words HE HELPS us every time.

So, how do you go to Jesus and hear what He has to say about your life?

1. READ the Bible!

It is simpler than you think. Just do a **B.U.R.P.**

- **B**IBLE: Read one or a few verses in the Bible
- **U**NDERSTAND: Ask yourself what you think it means
- **R**ESPOND: Apply it to your life
- **P**RAY: About the passage you have read and ask God to help you.

I often find that the part of the Bible I read doesn't necessarily help me on that particular day. Sometimes I make observations from what I read, but don't really think it will ever help me. But sooner or later, the things I read make more sense to me and when I am going through a particular situation, I am able to look back and remember what God said. Proverbs 2:1 says that we have a storehouse in us. Everything you see, hear and do, goes into that storehouse. It is like a massive computer chip that retains information (like cookies in the computer). Sooner or later the things you are listening to, reading and seeing will come out. If you fill your life with good stuff (like the Bible), then when the pressure is on, you will give out good stuff.

2. Listen to what the preacher says

I'll be the first to admit that sometimes listening to preaching is like listening and watching a miracle in action. HOW DO preachers manage to take the most amazing, exciting, humorous, mind-blowing stories (the Bible) and make it sound so boring?

The Bible teaches us that one of the key factors in the growth of the Church 2,000 years ago was that they devoted themselves to the leaders' teaching and preaching (read Acts 2). If you don't really know what Jesus is saying to you, why not take notes of what your pastor or youth pastor is talking about on Sunday or in the youth meeting and start to re-read the Bible passages used and apply it to your life.

3. Pray

Yeah, I know. The whole concept of talking to someone you can't see can be hard to do. The Bible says, *"Pray ... on all occasions ... "* (Ephesians 6:18). Prayer is so important that Jesus actually teaches us how to do it in Matthew 6:9–13. It is a model of prayer and knowing the model can really help you to organise your prayer time. A lot of people intend to pray, but when the time is available to them, they don't really know what to do and so it's easier not to bother. Jesus says, *"This, then, is how you should pray"* (v. 9):

► **FOCUS** *"Our Father in heaven"* (v. 9)
• Who are you talking to? Focusing your prayer helps you to stop thinking about your problems and helps you to focus on the one who not only gives answers, but IS the answer.

► **WORSHIP** *"hallowed be your name"* (v. 9)
• Spend some time worshipping God the next time you pray. Get out a worship CD, or just thank Him for aspects of His character. Worship helps you to change your mind

and takes your focus off yourself while placing it on God. The thing you magnify consumes you. If you constantly think about your problems, your problems will consume you. When you worship God, He becomes so huge in your thinking that you cannot help but realise that God can help you get through any situation and overcome any obstacle.

▶ **DECLARATION** *"your kingdom come, your will be done on earth as it is in heaven"* (v. 10)
- Here you are declaring, "God is the boss. I surrender my life to Him and allow Him to have His way." Remember that God is not a kill-joy, determined to take the fun out of life. Living for Jesus is flippin' brilliant. I have realised that if I say "no" to God, then I am responsible for the outcome of my life. Whereas if I say "yes" to God, HE is responsible for the outcome of my life. I know who I trust the most!
- You can even talk about some of the things you have just learned in the Bible. For example, if you read the verse, *"Be strong and courageous, because you will lead these people to inherit the land I swore to their forefathers to give them"* (Joshua 1:6), you may want to say to God, "God, help me to be strong and courageous in everything I do so that I can lead people into relationship with You."

▶ **NEED** *"Give us today our daily bread"* (v. 11)
- At this point, you are asking God for the things you need. It's Ok to ask God for wants too. When you are at a restaurant, not only do you eat what you need, but also what you want. Similarly, God loves to help you with needs and wants.

▶ **FORGIVENESS** *"Forgive us our debts, as we also have forgiven our debtors"* (v. 12)

- This is simply asking God to forgive you for your sin. The Bible also says in that verse that God forgives you as you have forgiven others. So through prayer, God reminds you of your need to forgive people for the wrong things they have done to you. Unforgiveness is like a sickness that eats away at people from the inside. Learn to forgive for your sake and God will also forgive you.

▶ **STRENGTH AND WISDOM** *"And lead us not into temptation, but deliver us from the evil one"* (v. 13)

- The evil one (devil) is hell-bent on your destruction. The Holy Spirit wants to strengthen you, so that you will have the courage not to sin. Likewise, He wants to give you wisdom for all areas of your life.

4. Talk to people you trust!

The Bible says,

> *"Where there is no counsel, the people fall;*
> *but in the multitude of counsellors there is safety."*
> (Proverbs 11:14, NKJV)

There should be people around you who you can trust to give you the right advice. (If there aren't, why not pray that God sends you some?) You can find wisdom from trusted people, from the "multitude of counsellors". Incidentally, the very fact that I am using the words "trusted people" means that they need to be the right people. For example, you may want to lose weight and therefore need to speak to a multitude of people to get advice. The local sumo wrestling convention has a multitude of people, but they may not have the best advice on calorie-controlled diets!

2. Jesus is FUN

The second reason why living for Jesus is flippin' brilliant is that Jesus is FUN!

I don't know what people are thinking when they tell me that my Bible is boring. My Bible is anything but boring. There are great stories in it, which PROVE that it's anything but boring!

- The one where a woman sticks a tent peg in a man's head! Aggressive maybe, but not boring! (Judges 4:21)
- The one where a great man lay on his side for a whole year! Less boring, just weird! (see Ezekiel 4)
- The one where the man has genitals like those of a donkey! (You can find that story in Ezekiel)

We have a generation of kids who think that the Bible is totally boring. These stories are hilarious, remarkable, bizarre and, at times, flummoxing!

The Bible is not boring at all! It is interesting and fun. Jesus was fun. Everywhere He went there were crowds of people walking with Him. Why? Because He was fun!

Two stories of Jesus and fun

▶ *Story 1*

Jesus' first miracle was at a wedding. The party went on for three days – now that's an impressive party. On the third day of the party there was a major catastrophe. The party hosts were running around in a panic saying, "Canaan, we have a problem!" The disciples come to Jesus and say, "Jesus, there's a problem." Jesus responds with something like, "What's wrong?"

- "Is someone crippled or mute?"..."NO"
- "Is someone deaf or blind?"..."NO"
- "Is someone nearly dead or dead?"..."NO"
- "Has the bride run off with the not-so-best man?"..."NO"

"Jesus! Will you listen? We've run out of booze!"
  "No booze?!"
  So Jesus turned some water into wine. Not just cheap stuff, but the best. No one was healed, or raised from the dead, but it was a great party!

▶ *Story 2*

The Bible talks about a time when there were 5,000 men plus women and children following Jesus, I reckon about 13,000 people. They've been following Him for about three days until Jesus asks, "I wonder if they're hungry?" I don't know about you, but I think that would be pretty obvious. I am hungry after half an hour, but these guys had followed Jesus around for days. Hadn't He noticed before?

  Jesus says to the disciples, "They are hungry. Let's feed them." "Feed them?" one gasps, "You must be joking. It would take a load of money to feed them; a year's wages at least!" So Jesus asks, "What do we have?" To which the disciples reply, "Just a little boy's lunch – five bits of bread and two fish." Now, contrary to sceptical opinion, this little dude was not carrying around with him two blue whales and a whole chain of bakery outlets! All he had was some bread and some fish.

Jesus prayed for the food and got the disciples to hand it out to everyone! As they handed out the food, it multiplied. There was so much that they were able to feed all the people AND there were twelve baskets of food left over.

I am not much of a chef, but I do know that if you put bread and fish together you have "fish fingers!" Yep, that's right, Jesus fed the masses with fish fingers. How cool is that?

There are many stories of how Jesus is fun, so if your theology or religion is telling you that Jesus isn't fun then you don't know the Jesus of the Bible. You know the Jesus who runs some drab kebab shop up the road, but you haven't got the Jesus of the Bible. He is committed to the Church having fun and He is committed to your fun. Now, you can have fun without having God in your life, but the time comes that at the end of all your fun, you still have to face your problems. With Jesus, your problems still exist but He grabs you by the hand and says, "I'm with you and I will help you through it!"

3. Jesus is your mate

The third reason why living for Jesus is flippin' brilliant is that the Bible says that, *"there is a friend who sticks closer than a brother''* (Proverbs 18:24). His name is Jesus.

A few years ago, my Mum travelled from Australia to visit me in England. I thought it would be great to treat her, so I took her to Paris, London and Cardiff. Over a five-day period we walked past tens of thousands of people. We saw thousands of people looking for the next best thing. We saw rich people, poor people, black and white people. We saw French, English, Welsh, African, Indian and Spanish people.

In amongst all that travel, the most content person I found was a little old lady living in a house in South Wales. She said to me, "Jesus is wonderful." "Why's that?" I asked. She replied, "I talk to Him like He's my friend. When I pray, I pull up an empty chair and imagine Him there. Yesterday the gas man was coming and I owed him £20. I didn't have £20, so I asked Jesus for the money. A while later the doorbell rang and I went to answer the door and Glyn, do you know what was there?" "Tell me," I said. "£20! There wasn't a person in sight, but there was £20!"

That lady had an understanding that Jesus was her friend and that He wants to help in any way He can. (He's your best friend too.)

4. Jesus forgets

The fourth reason why living for Jesus is flippin' brilliant is because Jesus forgets. It's not that Jesus has a bad memory and a good forgettery like many people I know, it's just that

Jesus CHOOSES to forget things! Listen to these words in the Bible:

> *"I, even I, am he who blots out*
> *your transgressions, for my own sake,*
> *and remembers your sins no more."*

(Isaiah 43:25)

Perhaps you carry hurt around with you from one day to the next, or maybe you can't forgive yourself for what you have done, or perhaps you can't forgive others for what they have done to you. When God is in your life, not only does He forget, but He helps the hurt you carry around with you to go away. In a recent conversation with a youth pastor, he was telling me that when he was young, a man sexually abused him. He said that later Jesus gave him the courage to forgive the man for what he had done. He said, "It's like the abuse never happened and when I think about it there's no hurt, no pain and no bitterness. God has made it like it never happened."

Whenever you sin, you can go to God and say, "I've done things my way and I've offended you. I know that because of my sin You had to die.[1] I'm sorry for what I have done." The Bible says, "God remembers no more." In other words, He forgets!

If you are reading this and you have messed up "big time", God will forgive you and help you beat it. Perhaps you go back to God again and again and say, "I'm sorry, I'm sorry, I'm sorry" and God says, "What? What? What? The first time you said sorry I threw it over that farthest mountain and I chose to remember no more." Jesus chooses to forget. Jesus doesn't judge your future by your past –

your destiny isn't determined by your history. Jesus is committed to your success. That's why He chooses to forget your sin. He can help you to get over your past mistakes and also what others may have inflicted on you. You may never forget it happened, but you won't carry around the hurt and pain any more.[2]

Finishing off the face-lift

Living for Jesus is flippin' brilliant: FACT! Let's go back to Paul's letter to the church in Ephesus to finish off the chapter AND convince you, once and for all, that what you are reading is truly truthfully true. (What???) Do you remember this?

> *"Now to him who is able to do immeasurably more than all we ask or imagine, according to his power that is at work within us..."*   (Ephesians 3:20)

One single mum raises her hand and says, "My daughter Lydia is ten years old. Next year she has to go to the temple to endure her years as a prostitute. Only in my wildest dreams can I IMAGINE that she doesn't have to go through that. Are you saying that she may not have to go to the temple after all?"

The reader repeats Paul's words, *"Now to him who is able to do immeasurably **more than all we ask or imagine**, according to his power that is at work within us..."*
"Yeah!"

I think the room would have gone ballistic. The young mum would have hugged her daughter and cried. Others would have cried – you probably would have cried too as you thought to yourself two things,

1. Wow, what a God!
2. Mental note to self: I hope someone writes about this in a book someday, called, *If I Had a Face Like Yours*!

Coming up:

"I'm a spaceship!"

Notes

1. God created the world perfect. When Adam sinned (Genesis 3), sin entered the world. Sin created a huge chasm between God and man. The only way that gap could be bridged was for Jesus to come, to die on the cross to take away the punishment of sin which is eternity in hell. When you ask God for forgiveness He remembers what His Son did on the cross and why He came to earth. He forgives, forgets and helps you to live a better, more fulfilled life!
2. Read *If I Was the Devil*, the first book in this series. It gives you more help on forgiving, forgetting and being all God called you to be.

Making it real for you!

1. Which point about Jesus do you like the most and why? (Local, Fun, Mate, Forgets)

   ....

   ....

   ....

2. Take some time to create a prayer journal to help you spend time with God every day. Have a look at the example below as a model for each day.
   (Don't forget to **B.U.R.P.**)

Date:	Details:
Bible verse (Write down the verses)	
Understand (What do you think it is saying?)	
Respond (How can you apply it to your life?)	
Pray • Focus • Worship • Declaration • Need • Forgiveness • Strength and courage	

Someone once said,

"If Barbie is so popular,
why do you have to buy
her friends?"

Face-lift #3

If I had a face like yours, I would . . .

. . . decide to be a spaceship!

In John 10:10, Jesus says,

> *"The thief comes only to steal and kill and destroy;*
> *I have come that they* [you] *may have life, and have it*
> *to the full."*

Jesus wants to **10–10** your life!

What an amazing boast Jesus is making here. It's the kind
of verse that makes you want to respond with two words!
The same two words you would say to me if I were to tell
you any of the following:

- I have a face like Brad Pitt
- I have the body of Mr Incredible
- I am the fastest man in the world
- I am the richest man in the world
- I am the greatest tennis player ever

To any of those statements you would say: PROVE IT! It's
not that you don't trust me, it's just that . . . well, you don't
trust me!

When Jesus makes this audacious statement in John 10:10 you just feel like shouting ... all together now ... PROVE IT!

So He does. In fact, the Gospel is all about Jesus proving that He came to give us life to the full. In other words the type of life where people are saying to you, *"I don't know what you're smoking, drinking, chewing or injecting, but I've gotta get me some of that!"*

The Bible records thirty miracles of Jesus (read John 21:25). Each miracle was Jesus proving that life to the full came from Him. The miracles all have corresponding relevance to us today, but let's investigate six of them.

1. The dude with the skin problem

In Matthew 8:1–3 we read the story of a man with leprosy. His problem wasn't just that he needed to visit the doctor to get some "dry skin repair cream", his problem was one of **isolation**.

The worst-case scenario with leprosy was that you would lose your sense of feeling. It was common that as a leper, if you cut yourself, you would not be able to feel it. Infection would then get into your wound and parts of your body would slowly rot away.

As soon as this man discovered he had leprosy, he literally had a death sentence placed over his head. He would no longer be able to cuddle his kids or kiss his wife. He would have been banished from his street, neighbourhood and community. He would have been sent away from everything he knew and loved and left to fend for himself.[1]

You may be the man with leprosy

I know there will be people reading this book who feel like they are on the outside of things, watching other people in society, church or youth have all the fun. Perhaps you are realising that you, just like the leper, are missing out. You feel like a face in the crowd, a number on a piece of paper, and one in six billion people. Perhaps you feel like you just DON'T BELONG! . . . stay tuned!

2. The girl with the biggest problem of all

In Matthew 9:18–19, 23–25 we read about a girl with a major problem – she was dead! She wasn't going to the movies tonight, shopping tomorrow or holidays in Spain next month. She was dead!

You may be that "dead girl"!

It is possible today to be part of the living dead (I don't mean to conjure up images of ghosts, zombies and ghouls!)

For some of you reading these pages, a part of you feels dead on the inside. Maybe you once felt alive to God, but now you feel a little bit dead on the inside. Perhaps you once felt alive in church and worship, but now you feel dead on the inside. Maybe you once felt alive in your relationships with parents or friends, but now you feel dead on the inside. Perhaps you once felt alive to your future and the possibilities of your life seemed endless and limitless, but

now as you look forward, you feel dead to your future! ...
Stay tuned!

3. The guy with double trouble!

In Mark 7:31–36, we read about a man who was deaf and
mute! If it wasn't bad enough that he couldn't hear, he
couldn't speak either! DOUBLE the TROUBLE; two for the
price of one!

You could be like the man with double trouble!

Just like the deaf man, you may have an inability to listen
to the right voice! You find there are people who think they
know best. Perhaps you run from one focus to another
because different people are telling you to do different
things with your life. Instead of becoming a person who
grows each day in the calling and gifting of God for your
life, you have become confused and distracted.

Perhaps you feel like your voice is drowned out in the
crowd. I wonder if you feel like you have something to say,
something to offer your church, friends or even family,
but you feel like no one is listening ... stay tuned!

4. The guy who isn't going places fast!

In Luke 5:17–26 we read about a man who is paralysed. This
guy is completely immobilised. He isn't getting to Pizza Hut

too easily. He needs some of his buddies to carry him and when they are not around, he isn't going anywhere.

You could be like the paralysed man!

Maybe you feel like you are not moving forward in your relationship with God. Perhaps you feel every time you take two steps forward, you take three steps back? Perhaps you make decisions to serve God at youth camps and conferences or even in church, but a few months later slide back into a life that is average and mediocre?

God's plan for you is a life of consistency. A life where you stand tall, shout loud and live large ... stay tuned!

5. The boy who's outta control

In Luke 9:37–45 we read about a little boy who is controlled by an evil spirit. What an unfortunate position to be in. This boy is alive, but he is often out of control. He is controlled by something and there is nothing he can do about it.

Maybe you are like this boy

Maybe there are areas of your life that seem out of control. I am not suggesting that you are demon-possessed, but perhaps there are certain things you wish you had control over. Maybe your life is controlled by greed, lust, selfish motivation or addictive behaviour. You have possibly even tried to break a particular behaviour pattern, but still find yourself going back to lifestyle or behaviour patterns that "control you" ... stay tuned!

6. The woman with the limp

In Luke 13:10–13 we read about a woman who was crippled. It didn't matter if she was walking, playing football or dancing at a party, she did it with a limp.

Maybe you are like the woman with the limp

Perhaps situations in life have left you with a limp. I'm not talking about a physical limp, I am referring to situations where once you had the ability to trust people, but over time people have let you down. There were times when you trusted implicitly, but you have been so disappointed that now you trust, but with a limp. It's just half-hearted trust. Maybe you trusted God once, but He didn't come through for you like you thought He should and so now you trust Him with a "not quite sure" kind of trust.

Perhaps you used to look forward to the future with hopes and dreams, but now, because of difficulty and trouble you look at your future with a limp. To you, it doesn't look so bright.

The spaceship story

Once, when I was in South Africa, my son Jaedon was approached by a friend who asked him a very interesting question. (Jaedon was two and a half at the time and he had been wearing a tracksuit top with the word "LEGEND" on the back.) My friend said, "Jaedon, are you a legend?"

Jaedon thought about it for a while and then replied, "No, I'm a spaceship!" We laughed, but it got me thinking . . .

Finishing of the face-lift

One of the greatest miracles of Jesus Christ can be summarised by,

- **Spaceship** and 10–10.

Jaedon was wearing clothes that labelled him, in this case, as a legend. My friend confirmed what the clothing said and asked Jaedon if it was indeed true that he was a legend.

In life, so many things label you. Your clothes label you as something; people label you as something else (through their words and actions towards you).

In that one small profound moment, Jaedon decided that he wasn't going to be what his clothes said he was and he certainly wasn't going to be labelled or defined by what someone called him. He wasn't having any of it. He wasn't a legend, he was a SPACESHIP!

One of the greatest miracles of Jesus is that you no longer need to be labelled or defined by things that have labelled and contained you for so long! Maybe you have been labelled by your past, your supposed future, your emotional or mental state, regrets, fears or failures. But Jesus comes and says, *"I have come that* [you] *may have life, and have it to the full"* (John 10:10).

We just read accounts of six people for whom Jesus did incredible miracles. He comes to the man with leprosy and says, "I have come to prove that I can give FULL, MAXIMUM, ABUNDANT life," and then healed him. That man had been known as "The man with leprosy" for a long time. He was defined by his leprosy, yet in a moment Jesus took away the very thing that labelled him. He was no longer, "The man with leprosy". He was now to be known as ... "The man"!

Similarly,

- "The dead girl" became just "the girl"
- "The deaf and mute man" became "the man"
- "The paralysed man" became "the man"
- "The boy with the evil spirit" became "the boy"
- "The crippled woman" became "the woman"

The great miracle of Jesus for you is that you no longer need to live your life defined and labelled. You are no longer dysfunctional, fat, a loser, forgotten, rich, poor, smart, stupid, black, white, the son of your father or daughter of your mother, a widow, alone. You are no longer just the result of life's circumstance. You are now,

- The man, the woman, the kid, the boy, the girl.

When Jesus says, *"I've come to give you life to the full"*, it means that you are no longer defined by what's happened to you, but rather by "whose" you are!

The Bible says in John 1:12,

> *"To all who received him, to those who believed in his name, he gave the right to become children of God!"*

Who are you? You are a child of God and that means that God gives you the power to become the person He destined you to be.

You are not a legend, you are a spaceship!

Coming up:

"RIOT at the game!"

Note

1. Leprosy carried with it the great fear that it was contagious. All lepers were banished from the community and left either to fend for themselves, or join a community of other lepers.

Making it real for you!

1. How have people labelled you?

   ....
   ....
   ....

2. Why is it so difficult living life with a label?

   ....
   ....
   ....

3. In an ideal world, what would you really like to be like?

   ....
   ....
   ....

4. What aspect of your life currently stops you from being the "spaceship" God wants you to be?

   ....
   ....
   ....

5. Take a few moments to talk to God and ask Him to help you to throw off people's labels so you can live the life God intended!

   ....
   ....
   ....

Someone once said,

"I tried sniffing coke once,
but the ice cubes got stuck
up my nose!"

Face-lift #4

If I had a face like yours, I would...

...*choose enthusiasm*

Back in 2003, the final of the Rugby World Cup took place between Australia and England. I was born in England, but I was raised in Australia. My family still live in Australia, my wife is Australian and I even have an Australian passport. However, I was supporting England! The final score was 21–21 and it then went into extra time. I was fearful and worried at the same time. I didn't really care about winning; I just wanted to have boasting rights! I wanted to be able to send SMSs and emails to my buddies in Australia saying, "**LOSERS** – We won!" I couldn't stand the tension. With about a minute left, Johnny Wilkinson kicked a drop goal and England won the game. I ran around the house like a lunatic, jumping off the walls, hugging people, shouting and doing the "dance of joy"! We were all shouting, "We won! We won! We won! We won!" But the truth is we didn't win, we just watched. Fifteen boys in Sydney put on a white shirt with a red rose and played the game. They won. We just watched.

Jesus didn't die on the cross for us to be watchers. He didn't die on the cross for a generation of churchgoers to watch people go to hell. In Corinthians, Paul says, "Run the race and run to win" (see 1 Corinthians 9:24). I have heard various people (friends, well-meaning PE teachers and spectators) say, "Winning isn't everything. It's the taking part that counts!" The person who invented that phrase was obviously a loser. When you run a race, you don't run thinking, "I don't want to win. I CHOOSE TO LOSE." Your plan is to WIN!

People who don't know God should look at you and say, *"I don't know what you are smoking, drinking, chewing or injecting, but I have gotta get me some of that!"* When you hear people saying that to you (or words like that), surely we are starting to WIN a nation again!

Understanding reverence

Some people think that being overly enthusiastic shows a lack of reverence, but there is a genuine misunderstanding of the term "reverence". We often mistake that word to mean "being quiet". That is merely part of the whole truth.

The Bible says that God is "lifted up with shouts of praise" (see Psalm 47:5). He lives in our shout. If I was the devil (good name for a book!) I would stick a dummy (pacifier) in your mouth. If I was the devil, I'd say to the Church, "Shut up, sit down and keep quiet."

It's time for the Church to get its shout back! It's time to "spit the dummy", because God lives in the shout and one of the keys to living life the way God intended is **enthusiasm**.

The dictionary says that enthusiasm means to, "rave, to go into raptures and to go overboard". When did you last see a church rave, go into raptures and go overboard?

Paul's letter to the church in Ephesus

Ephesians 1:1 says, *"To the saints in Ephesus, the faithful in Christ Jesus . . . "* (A quick recap of Face-lift #1 will remind you of the facts about the city of Ephesus.)

When Paul says these words, he is reminding the Ephesians that . . .

- They live in Ephesus having been born in Ephesus
- They are accustomed to the customs and culture of Ephesus
- Their way of life includes fear, worry, murder, prostitution and unhappiness.

But he is also showing them that now as Christians they have a new way of life and that new way of life is "in Christ". Thirty-six times in the book of Ephesians Paul says, you are "in Christ", "in God", etc.

The word "enthusiasm" has the prefix "enthus" or "*en theos*" in the Greek. "*En theos*" means – are you ready for it? – "IN GOD". So when we talk about being enthusiastic, we are not just talking about something that is cultural to Americans or Englishmen at football games, we are talking about the natural state of affairs for anyone who calls themselves a Christian. To be enthusiastic as a Christian is not an option. It is MANDATORY and will inevitably cause people to say, *"Whatever you are smoking, drinking, chewing or injecting, I gotta get me some of that!"*

A theologian by the name of R. A. Torrey said, "God dwells in a perpetual state of enthusiasm." [1] In other words, God always raves, He always goes into raptures and He always goes overboard!

Look at creation! He didn't quit at day four, He had days five and six to complete and in the middle of it all He made a giraffe! He made a gnat and He made a bulldog. He made a porcupine! He was raving and rapturous and definitely going overboard.

What did Jesus Christ do on the cross if He wasn't raving, going into raptures and going overboard? He could've come at a time when execution was simple – a quick spear through the heart? No, Jesus went overboard.

The time I got mad (once, twice, thrice)

Once

Recently in one of our church services a man approached me at the end of the service and said, "I am a watchman!" Now I think I knew what he meant, but I played dumb and said, "Oh, you make watches do you?" He didn't smile and I knew I was in for it. He continued with, "These people are jumping around like idiots." He was referring to the fact that people jump during the fast songs in praise and worship.

"Idiots?" I said, "Do you see that sixteen-year-old boy jumping up and down in worship? He had no friends and was hooked on drugs, but God got hold of his life and he is now free of drugs and has loads of friends in church. He also has purpose and destiny to live for."

"Did you see that married couple with their hands raised in worship? Before they became Christians they were having affairs. They nearly got divorced and it looked likely that a fierce custody battle would take place over who would get to keep their children. But they let God change them. They now love each other more than ever and their kids love coming to church to worship God."

"Do you see that young woman over there? An uncle abused her when she was young and she carried the hurt and bitterness around with her. She had a complete inability to love anyone because of her pain, but God helped her and everything is different now."

I turned to the critic and said, "So, who are you to say that these people are jumping around like idiots? They are enthusiastic and passionate in worship because their God is not just a figment of their imagination. He is not a stained glass window or a far, distant deity. He is real. He has picked them up, healed their hurts and they can't help but respond to God in a way that is full of passion and enthusiasm."

I was pretty ticked off!

It was a good answer to a man who knew about "God – the theory", but had no understanding of "God – the One who raves, goes into raptures and goes overboard."

Twice

Another time I had a gentleman come up to me at church and say, "The problem with your church is you smile too much!" I looked at him and said, "The problem with your church is you frown too much!"

Thrice

Again another time, a professional Christian critic said to me, "The problem with your church is that you emphasise the offering." I said, "What do you mean? We emphasise everything. We emphasise the cleanliness of the building – you weren't here at 8:00am when guys were sweeping out the gutters on the street outside. We emphasise the welcome – that's why seven or eight people shook your hand before you got to your seat. We emphasise the coffee – it's good coffee. We emphasise the worship – that's why the band is here every Thursday night rehearsing. We emphasise the preaching – that's why we prepare so well in the Word of God." And then I said to him, "My question to you, sir, is why do *you* emphasise the offering?"

There are three things you need to know about enthusiasm:

1. Enthusiasm is not a feeling, it's a discipline

One of the saddest things I see as I travel is leaders and Christians who look so sad. They look beaten. They display an attitude and a demeanour that shows they've given up because life and leadership are tough. Every time I see a person like that I wonder what happened to them. As I walk away my prayer is always, "God, don't let that happen to me. I don't mind bad news and I don't mind being in the valley (Psalm 23), because I know during those times that Your rod and Your staff are with me. So God, I choose not to allow hurt and disappointment to stay in my heart and fester."

If you wait until you feel enthusiastic, you will only be enthusiastic sometimes, while at other times you will not. In the Old Testament, David, and other men and women of

God, didn't *feel* like being enthusiastic, but they literally had to grab themselves by the scruff of the neck and say, "Be enthusiastic!" (Psalms 13; 31; 34; Habakkuk 3).

Enthusiasm and discipline in being enthusiastic are found in one thing and that is: what God has done for you! Sometimes it's good just to sit down and think through the things God has done for you. When you do that, you can't help but end up living enthusiastically for Him because you remember that He has:

- Said He will always be with you (Hebrews 13:5)
- Promised good things to happen to you (Philippians 1:6)
- Answered your prayers (2 Corinthians 1:10–11)
- Promised to hear you when you talk to Him (Psalm 17:6)
- Amazing plans and purposes for your life (Jeremiah 29:11)
- Promised to give you life to the full (John 10:10)
- Proven that He does miracles (John 21:25)
- Proven to millions of others on the planet that living for Him is flippin' brilliant

Charles Spurgeon[2] once said, "Faith shuts its eyes at difficulties, it laughs at impossibilities and cries 'It shall be done!' "[3] I love that statement. It is a statement that is based on you not living a life of faith based on emotion, but rather, a life of discipline.

John Wesley's diary

Look at the diary of John Wesley:

- Sunday, a.m., May 5 – Preached in St. Anne's. Was asked not to come back any more.

- Sunday, p.m., May 5 – Preached in St. John's.
  Deacons said, "Get out and stay out."
- Sunday, a.m., May 12 – Preached in St. Jude's.
  Can't go back there, either.
- Sunday, a.m., May 19 – Preached in St. Somebody Else's.
  Deacons called special meeting and said I couldn't return.
- Sunday, p.m., May 19 – Preached on street.
  Kicked off street.
- Sunday, a.m., May 26 – Preached in meadow.
  Chased out of meadow as bull was turned loose during service.
- Sunday, a.m., June 2 – Preached out at the edge of town.
  Kicked off the highway.
- Sunday, p.m., June 2 – Preached in a pasture.
  Ten thousand people came out to hear me.

Now that's discipline! If Wesley had been "feeling-based" enthusiastic about his God-given calling of preaching to people and seeing them give their lives to Jesus, then he would have given up and 10,000 people would never have turned up to hear him speak about Jesus.

2. Enthusiasm catches up with your face and your body

The second thing about enthusiasm is that it catches up with your face.

I love leading weddings. I love standing at the front and helping to make the groom feel at ease. I say to him, "Are you sure she's the right one?" and other such questions to really make him nervous on the morning of the wedding (I know it's cruel, but it's also fun). We all stand as the bride walks down the aisle and I must admit, I've never seen a miserable bride. I've seen brides cry, but it's always been a happy cry! (A note for the girls: we men don't understand that! If you cry we think you're sad so don't confuse us. Crying = sad. Smiling = happy. Ok? Please learn it, it will really help us A LOT!)

I've never seen a bride walk down the aisle and turn round and say, "Hey! I didn't invite you! On your bike – clear off, you waster!" I've never seen a bride slap the groom when she gets to the altar because he is wearing the wrong flower and it clashes with the bridesmaids' dresses.

- She's happy, she's got the man of her dreams.
- He's happy, he's going on honeymoon!
- Dad's happy, he doesn't have to pay for his daughter's clothes any more.
- Mum is happy (hopefully), because the daughter is marrying the right man.
- The crowd is happy, because the "knees up" later on should be a beauty!
- Everyone's happy and it shows.

In the Bible, it says that we are the bride of Christ (Revelation 21:2).

- I think our worship's got to let it show.
- I think our preaching's got to let it show.
- I think the way you go about your life has got to let it show.

- You see, enthusiasm catches up with your face and your body.

The mandatory football story

I take my wife to football (soccer) matches. I'm a Manchester City supporter and so is she. She has no choice. My children have been indoctrinated; they are Man City supporters too! Once at a Premiership football game,[4] we were unable to get tickets to sit with the Man City fans[5] and so we sat with 47,000 opposition fans. On the way to the game, I said to Sophia, "There are some rules I need to explain for this game because if you do something wrong, I'm a dead man!"

> **Rule 1:** If City scores then we are **sad on the outside** but **happy on the inside**.

> **Rule 2:** If the opposition scores then we are **happy on the outside** and **sad on the inside**.

We spent time rehearsing it. She is intelligent, she married me! But at the game, something happened! As City started to push towards the goal my wife started to get excited. I tried to hold her back, but when City scored my wife stood to her feet and shouted, "Yeah!" There was nearly a riot at the game!

She's caught the truth though. If you're enthusiastic then you can't keep it in. If you say to me, "Glyn, I'm enthusiastic on the inside," but look miserable on the outside, I will say to you, "You are a liar, sir, because enthusiasm always catches up with your face and your body."[6]

3. It makes you do anything regardless of what the critics think

In John 14 we read about Peter and the other disciples. They are in a boat in a storm and the Bible says that they see "something" walking towards them on the water. They think it's a ghost when all of a sudden somebody says, "Hey, it's not a ghost. It's Jesus!"

Peter says "Jesus, if it's You out there, tell me to come out on the water with You!" So Jesus says, "Come on!" Peter gets up and gets ready to walk on the water towards Jesus. (Remember there's a storm.) Imagine what is going through the minds of all the other disciples in the boat:

- Thomas is saying, "I doubt it!" (he was Mr Sceptical).
- Bartholomew is saying, "Go on, you can do it!" (he was Mr Encourager).
- Judas is saying, "We could make some money out of this!" (he was Mr Greedy).

In the midst of everything, Peter didn't think, "I'm about to do the impossible." He just said, "I'm coming Jesus!" and he started to walk on the water.

- The Bible says that Peter began to sink (don't be too hard on the lad, remember, there's a storm), at which point Jesus picks up Peter and they begin to chat. Now let's just pause the DVD right there. Where are they having this conversation? On the water!

The Bible says, *"when they got back in the boat . . . "* Note that the Bible doesn't say **how long** it was before they got back in the boat, it just says **when** they got back in the boat. So, at the very least, they walked back to the boat together, while at the very most Jesus could have taken Peter for a stroll on the water before returning to the boat! Even though Peter failed, when he took the hand of Jesus, he learned to walk on water again! (If you have failed in something recently, Jesus wants to take your hand and help you achieve great things too!)

Here's the point I'm trying to make: Peter's mentality was simple. He said, "I'd rather be with Jesus in the storm doing the impossible than safe here in my comfort zone. I don't care what you guys (the boys in the boat) think, Jesus is out there, so that's where I'm going!"

You may have heard it said that Peter walked on water because of his faith. I think maybe that's true, but it's not the whole truth. I think he walked on water because he was enthusiastic. Everything about Peter's life was characterised by enthusiasm. Whether it was denying Jesus (Luke 22:34) or chopping someone's ear off (John 18:26), whatever he was doing, he did it enthusiastically.

You see, you thought it was faith that made him walk on water, but my dictionary tells me that to be enthusiastic means:

• to rave, to go into raptures and to go *overboard*. (What did Peter do if he didn't go "OVERBOARD"? Remember, he was in a boat!)

Finishing the face-lift

So what do you think? What would happen if every Christian on the planet lived a life of enthusiasm? I can't help but think that more people would say, *"I don't know what you are smoking, drinking, chewing or injecting, but I gotta get me some of that!"* Enthusiasm is a choice! The choice is yours ... I think your face would do well to live ... enthusiastically!

Coming up:

"They saw me naked!!!'

Notes

1. Source unknown. Some attribute this saying to A. W. Tozer.
2. Charles H. Spurgeon (1834–1892) was an English Baptist preacher, author, and editor. Pastor of the Metropolitan Tabernacle (London) from 1861 until his death.
3. Extract from Spurgeon's sermon "The soul winner".
4. The top football league in Britain.
5. The fans of opposing teams are always segregated due to "Passion", which is often displayed as aggression and invariably results in fighting. There will always be occasions when you are desperate to see your team play, but you are unable to get tickets to sit with the rest of "your fans". What do you do? You buy a ticket to sit with the other supporters and tell yourself not to cheer when your team scores a goal. What happens when your team scores? Invariably you forget your plan, stand to your feet and cheer ... usually regretting that outward display of enthusiasm as you are escorted from the stadium for your own protection.
6. Read the story of the man who got healed in Acts 3. He took enthusiasm into church and it was deemed as an appropriate response to what Jesus had done.

Making it real for you!

1. How would you define reverence and how have you lived with a mistaken understanding of reverence?

   ....
   ....
   ....
   ....

2. If enthusiasm is a discipline, when do you need to be more disciplined in your enthusiasm?

   ....
   ....
   ....
   ....

3. If enthusiasm catches up with your face and your body, how can you better show everyone that living for Jesus is flippin' brilliant?

   ....
   ....
   ....
   ....

4. If enthusiasm makes you do anything regardless of what the critics think, in what areas of your life do you need to decide not to hold back any longer?

   ....
   ....
   ....
   ....

Someone once said,

"What happens if you get scared half to death twice?"

Face-lift #5

If I had a face like yours, I would...

...GO then LEAVE!

Acts 16:16–40 tells a brilliant story! (Page 978 in my Bible!)
Verse 16 says, *"Once when we were going to the place of
prayer..."* My life has been full of "once I was going to"
moments! For example...

- Once I was going to do Tae Kwon Do, but I didn't like
  bowing to the flag, so I quit.
- Once I was going to be a ballerina! Then I slapped
  myself across the face and realised it was only a bad
  dream
- Once I was going to be single! But then I got married.

The phrase, *"once we were going to"* is the start of
something very ordinary. This was meant to be an ordinary
day for Paul. They weren't expecting any great thing to
take place, in fact, they were just "boring" Christians who
decided to go and pray (perhaps they used the **B.U.R.P.**
technique!). Even though this was an ordinary start to a
very ordinary day, something out of the ordinary
happened.

Recently, I was driving in a car with a friend. I wasn't
expecting anything life-changing to happen, but it did. God

began to speak to me! I don't know how God speaks to you, but He speaks to me in a very simple way. When I was a kid, my Dad used to play a game with me. He would hide something in the house and tell me to go and find it. The further away from the object I was, Dad would say, "Cold, colder, colder..." but as I got closer to the hidden object, Dad would say, "Hot, hotter, hotter, hotter" until I was right next to it and then Dad would say, "Your pants are on fire!" and sure enough, there was the hidden treasure, usually buried under the towels on the second shelf of the linen cupboard!

God speaks to me the same way. I usually don't hear an audible voice or see an angelic visitation (big word meaning an angel appearing in front of you). I usually feel hot in my heart, almost like the feeling of nerves before you bungee jump. Jeremiah says this in the Old Testament,

> *"But if I say, 'I will not mention him*
> *or speak any more in his name,'*
> *his word is in my heart like a fire,*
> *a fire shut up in my bones.*
> *I am weary of holding it in;*
> *indeed, I cannot."*   (Jeremiah 20:9)

That is exactly how I feel when God is speaking to me. I feel HOT in my heart and I know that the thoughts I am thinking are a result of God directing my thoughts and speaking to me. And so recently, at the start of an ordinary day, expecting no great thing to happen, God began to speak to me. With God, there is no such thing as ordinary. God can take the most ordinary day and make it the most exciting. With God, anything can happen!

In Acts 16:16, Paul is at the start of a very ordinary day, when, *"we were met by a slave girl who had a spirit by which she predicted the future. She earned a great deal of money for her owners by fortune-telling."* The Bible says that she harangued[1] them for three days! She followed them and preached at them and complained to them and was a pain in the big toe! Paul finally got so annoyed with her that he cast out the demon! The girl was really happy. Paul was even happier because he no longer had this girl following him around everywhere. Everyone was really happy except for...

1. the demon that went back to hell, and,
2. the owners of the girl who could no longer make money out of her!

The Bible says that Paul and Silas (his buddy) were taken in front of the authorities by the owners of the slave girl, lied about, accused and stripped naked! Then they were severely flogged, thrown into the inner jail where they experienced an earthquake and finally, verse 40 says, *"Then they left!"* (So much for an ordinary day!)

Verse 16 starts with, *"once we were going ... "* and the end of the story says, *"Then we left!"* Similarly, life is about,

• "Going to" and "leaving from".

Life is all about the seasons (Ecclesiastes 3:1) that you either endure or embrace, but it is important that you "go to" and "leave from" – i.e. that you don't **stay put**! "Going to" and "leaving from" is not always a quick transaction. Time lapses when you "go to" a new season of life. But it is what you do in that season that determines,

- How you leave, and,
- What new season of life you go into.

Paul and Silas did three main things after this ordinary day got a little bit interesting. Three important things that will help you face any day with your head (face) held high:

1. Pray (see vv. 16 and 25)

The Bible says in verse 16 that they were *"going to the place of prayer"*. It doesn't, however, actually say they arrived at the place of prayer. On their way they met a demon-possessed girl. It is important to remember that the devil wants to stop you from praying! Prayer creates a space where you can hear from God and when you hear from God, amazing things can happen.

When I was in the car with my friend, my heart began to burn hot and I knew God was speaking to me. I really felt God say that He wanted me to take an event we run and host it in a remote venue. I shared the thought with my friend and he agreed with me that it didn't make sense. That night, I shared the "God-thought" with some other people where one said that he knew the exact place and how it could best work there. That conversation led to another with other people across the country, which led to a series of miracles and more in the pipeline! The devil wants to rob you of moments like that!

And God said ... "and it was so"

In Genesis 1 it says,

- *"And God said, 'Let there be light,' and there was light"* (v. 3).
- *"And God said, 'Let there be an expanse between the waters to separate water from water.' ... And it was so"* (vv. 6–7).
- *"And God said, 'Let the water under the sky be gathered to one place ...' And it was so"* (v. 9).

And it continues in the following pattern, "And God said ... and it was so" throughout Genesis chapter 1.

It is a brilliant principle, because whatever God says, happens. The reason the devil doesn't want you to hear from God is because he hates the fact that whatever God says, happens.

Nearly clever scientists

God is able to make things *ex nihilo* (out of nothing).[2] Even the cleverest scientists need something in order to turn it into something else. Only God can take nothing and make something!

Once upon a time, the nearly clever scientists said to God, "We don't need You any more. We can make anything just like You! You are out of a job; it is time to let us clever scientists take charge." "Really?" God said. "Are you ready for a duel then?" He asked. To which the nearly clever scientists replied, "Anything You can do, we can do better!" So God said, "I challenge you to make a man, just like I did in the beginning of time. But there is one rule; you have to use what I used in the beginning. You have to use dust!" To which the nearly clever scientists responded, "No problem, God!" As the nearly clever scientists bent down to pick up some dust, God shouted, "Oi, get your own dust!"[3]

Only God can take nothing and make something. Perhaps you look at your future and see nothing. Perhaps you think nothing or are feeling nothing. The brilliant thing about God is that when He speaks, He can make something awesome out of nothing (take a look at the universe for proof!).

The non-negotiables

Non-negotiables are best defined as things you have to do. For example, if you are a student and you are required to be in an exam at 9:00am, then that is a non-negotiable. If your friend rings you and says, "Fancy a coffee?" you say, "No, I have an exam." OR, if you have eaten some dodgy meal and feel the compulsion to run to the bathroom, that is also non-negotiable. If your friend stops you on the way to the bathroom and suggests you catch a movie, you are not going to change your plans and go to the cinema immediately, because visiting the bathroom is something you MUST DO ... or else!

Somehow, you have to learn to make prayer a non-negotiable. Perhaps you have had times when you were going to pray and then your phone rang and you answered it instead, or you walked past the TV and saw the "A-Team" was showing as a re-run and so sat down to watch it. Prayer for you has become a negotiable. Something you do if you can find the time or have no better option.

Prayer is the place you hear, "And God said..." and then all you have to do is wait for the "...and it was so..." But if you haven't heard the "...and God said..." then your expectancy that God can and will do great things is severely diminished and Christianity becomes ... ***boring***!

2. Praise (see v. 25)

Psalm 34:3 says,

> *"Oh, magnify the LORD with me,*
> *And let us exalt His name together."* (NKJV)

I don't know about you, but if I had been through everything Paul and Silas had been through, I don't know how interested in prayer and praise I would be! Paul decided to focus on the answer (God) and not the problem because he knew that the thing you magnify consumes you (Psalm 34:3).

Paul chose not to be negative. Negatives belong in a dark room, but as children of God we are meant to live in the light (Ephesians 5:8). So, in the middle of a dreadful situation, Paul and Silas began to sing and praise God! As they sang, the foundations of the jail began to shake, the chains fell off and the doors flew open.

When you are going through a difficult time, you need to pray and praise because that's how the chains will fall off and the gates will open. In other words, something happens! The very things that were holding Paul and Silas back (in this case the chains and doors within the prison cell) were destroyed and Paul and Silas were able to walk free. The Bible says in Galatians 5:1 that, *"It is for freedom that Christ has set us free."* In other words, although you may feel "locked up" during tough times, prayer and praise make room for God to come into your situation and help you.

3. They left!

Verse 40 says *" ... Then they left."* In a nutshell, the story goes like this:

- "Once we were going to ... then it all went wrong ... then we left ... "

It doesn't say that Paul and Silas...

- Were angry about their treatment
- Sat in a counselling session and said, "Pastor, you don't understand what they did to me! They lied about me, called me rude words ... **they even saw me naked!**"
- Endured long hours of prayer and fasting in order to get over what they had been through.

NO, none of that. They just LEFT.

Some of you need to leave. I don't mean leave your church. I mean leave the past in the past and the hurt of the other day in the other day! Your heritage is not your destiny. The things that have brought you to this point in your life have merely been a vehicle to get you to where you are right now. It is unfortunate that bad stuff happens along the way. Paul and Silas endured horrific torture on their journey. It was a tough day and yet they just left. Perhaps you need to pray, praise and leave yesterday where it is. Move on!

In verse 33, the very people who were against Paul and Silas were the same ones who ended up helping them. If you face challenges with people in your life, then why not pray, praise and then move on. You may find that those very people you are having difficulty with end up becoming your greatest friends.

Finishing the face-lift!

Imagine you lived in Ephesus. Imagine you had lived a life full of fear, worry, murder and prostitution. The effects that would have on you could potentially be devastating. How do you move on and live a life of influence, success and significance without your history and hurt holding you back? You just pray, praise and then you leave. You don't leave geographically, but you make the decision with God to leave the past where it is and not to revisit it time and time again. Or, as Paul puts it in Ephesians,

> "... *put on the full armour of God, so that when the day of evil comes* [those days when you are tempted to look over your shoulder and live under the threat of your past], *you may be able to stand your ground, and after you have done everything, to stand.*"
>
> (Ephesians 6:13)

Coming up:

"It's all gone Pete Tong!"

Notes _____

1. Harangued; meaning to lecture someone at length in an aggressive and critical manner.
2. God made the universe out of nothing.
3. Source unknown.

Making it real for you!

1. Why should prayer be such an important part of your life?

   ....
   ....
   ....

2. What three things can you do to make prayer a non-negotiable?

   (a) ....
   (b) ....
   (c) ....

3. What is the focus of praise during difficult times and how does it help you?

   ....
   ....
   ....

4. Have you left the past behind? What areas of your past do you need to move on from?

   ....
   ....
   ....

5. Take a few moments to pray, asking God to help you move on from your past, so that you like Paul can say, "Once I was going to ... and then I left ..."

Someone once said,

"Those who think they
know everything, annoy those
of us who do."

Face-lift #6

If I had a face like yours, I would ...

... ignore the facts

- If you are a lawyer, it would be a bad idea to ignore the facts!
- If you are a policeman, it would be a bad idea to ignore the facts!
- If you own a house and it is falling down, it would be a bad idea to ignore the facts!
- If you are in a boat and it is filling with water, it would be a bad idea to ignore the facts!
- If you have a toothache, it would be a bad idea to ignore the facts!

HOWEVER, if you love God, it would be a very good idea to ignore the facts. Let me explain what I mean.

In the Bible there is a very big difference between "fact" and "truth". The facts speak of what you are experiencing at the moment, but they do not always reflect the truth of what the future possibly holds. This is true in life:

- Disneyland has many great roller-coasters. The truth is, they are great roller-coasters. The fact however, is you may not enjoy them. Fact and truth are two different things.

- The truth is, it's freezing outside. The fact is you might not feel it because you are used to arctic temperatures.
- The truth is, there are plenty of houses for sale where you live. The fact is you may not be able to find one to buy.

When it comes to the life God has for you, the fact of what you are currently experiencing may not reflect the truth of what you can potentially experience. This chapter is dedicated to you experiencing everything God has for your life. In other words, you can change the facts, so the facts reflect the truth. (Needless to say, the result it will have on your face is "lifting".)

For many years, the Church has preached the truth but hasn't lived the facts. People have looked at the Church and said, "You are preaching it, but you're not living it! You preach about prosperity and joy, but you're the most miserable people in the world!" It's time to change that!

John 21: Fact and truth

In John 21 we read a great story. Why not take a moment to read the first fourteen verses. Verse 1 says, *"It happened this way"*, which is a classic way of saying, "Once upon a time". This story takes place when Jesus had just died and risen again. He had appeared to some of the disciples, so there must have been some strange rumours circulating about Him. You can imagine two neighbours (N1 and N2) gossiping over the fence:

[N1]: "I heard that Jesus is back!"

[N2]: "Which Jesus? The one who runs the kebab shop?"

[N1]: "No, the one from Nazareth!"

[N2]: "What, the one who died?"

[N1]: "Yeah, Him!"

[N2]: "HELLLLOOOOOOO! If He's dead, how can He be back?"

[N1]: "I dunno, but Bart was telling me he saw Him!"

[N2]: "Oh yeah, and I suppose Bart has been out on the razz [1] again?"

[N1]: "No seriously, he reckons that Jesus rose from the dead!"

[N2]: "And you believe him?"

[N1]: "I dunno. A bit weird though!"

[N2]: "Yeah. Well, if He's back, I hope He doesn't bring my mother-in-law back to life like He did for Peter. What a shocker that was. And Peter thought Jesus was his friend!"

[N1]: "Yeah, I know what you mean. Later pal!"

[N2]: "Later mate!"

In the story, all the disciples are gathered together. Simon Peter, the unofficial leader, decided to go fishing and all the others decided to go too. Despite many of them being professional fisherman, the Bible says they fished all night and caught nothing (so much for professional)! Early the next morning, Jesus stood on the shore, but the disciples didn't realise it was Him. He called out to them and said, *"Friends, haven't you caught any fish?"* They replied *"No!"* And so Jesus suggested that they *"... throw their nets on the right side of the boat."*

When they did this, they ended up with a huge catch of fish. The penny dropped and they realised it was Jesus talking, so Peter put his clothes back on (v. 7) and swam towards Jesus (Yeah, I know what you are thinking. Most people take their clothes off to swim, but not Peter. Odd, don't you think?).

Four facts about the disciples in the boat

Fact 1: They had a past life

James and John (two of Jesus' disciples) and their father Zebedee, owned a fishing company: "Zeb and Sons Fishy Dishes"![2] Peter had also been a fisherman before Jesus asked him to follow Him. Fishing was Peter, James and Johns' livelihood. It was their "past life".

"Past life" is best defined as, "a way of life that you are accustomed to". I am accustomed to various ways of life . . .

- I'm accustomed to being a son. I know how to do that because I have parents. My mum helped me to learn the duck and weave technique of avoiding her slaps. I would duck and weave around her. By the time I was twelve I had perfected the duck and weave technique and that made me a good rugby player!
- I am accustomed to being a student; reading books, doing dissertations and missing my planned deadlines despite staying up all night to try and meet them.

- I am accustomed to dating! I wasn't always married! The chat-up line, "Hey babe, you didn't fall out of the ugly tree," is a line I tried from time to time. (You're right, it didn't work!)
- I'm also accustomed to being a husband, father, pastor, preacher, coach, friend...

A way of life is not so much what you do, it's more who you are. It's your mindsets and thought patterns. It's your attitudes and your comfort zones. The amazing thing about past life is that it's easy to slip back into.

Fact 2: They reverted to their old way of life

The disciples went back to their comfort zone. Peter says "I'm going fishing." Peter is saying that, "Everything's gone wrong with Jesus. We had great dreams but they haven't come true. Everything's gone pear-shaped so I'm going to go back to what I know."

- Fact: they had a past life!
- Fact: so do you. A way of life that you run back to when tough times come, instead of running to God.

I was in Australia recently. In case you didn't realise, I am a man. I have a wife, children, mortgage payments and plenty of other adult responsibilities, but when I'm in Australia with my mum, I revert back to being a sixteen-year-old. There's something about seeing my mum that makes me want to tease her. I want to be a naughty little, practical joke-playing boy again. It's a way of life I'm accustomed to.

All too often, just like the disciples, in times of crisis, we revert back to old ways of thinking, acting and living instead of moving forward in passionate pursuit of our destiny! That's why the book of Ephesians was written. Ephesus was a city of darkness and of demonic curses. Paul (the writer of Ephesians), knew they had been through abuse and lived with fear, but then as Christians, when things got difficult, they reverted back to their old way of life. They kept saying incantations and wearing lucky charms. Paul wrote telling them: "Don't do it!" They needed to get out of their old ways.

Fact 3: The disciples were going through emotional turmoil

Have you ever been through a time when everything seems to be going great, when suddenly everything goes "Pete Tong"?[3] You hear yourself say, "What's going on?" That is exactly what happened to the disciples.

- Their best friend, Judas, betrayed Jesus
- Judas killed himself
- Jesus was publicly humiliated
- Jesus was killed.

It's all gone "Pete Tong". The story in John 21 is one of aimlessness and purposelessness. They've gone back to the usual routine of working 9–5 (or whatever hours fisherman work). Going to bed, waking up, doing the 9–5 routine and then doing it all again tomorrow.

They were repeating the same cycle that you may be caught up in. Asking questions like,

- What do I have to live for?
- What's the purpose of my life?
- Where's it all leading?

This is what had happened with the disciples. They lost everything in a moment and didn't know what the future held.

Fact 4: They caught nothing!

They didn't catch a thing. No fish, not even a tiny little one, absolutely nothing! The disciples would have been thinking, "If all else fails, at least we know how to fish!" And so they went from where they were, back to what they knew ... but they caught nothing.

Whenever you go back to a way of life you've been accustomed to because it's your comfort zone; because it is too "stretching" to stay where you are, you will catch nothing! God's plan is not for you to go back, but for you to move forward (see Proverbs 15:24). God wants you to move on in grace, in knowledge, in strength, in power, in commitment, in encouragement. That's God's plan.

What did Peter get for his efforts? You can imagine him saying,

- I've got nothing
- I've got no business
- I've got no mentor
- I've got no hopes
- I've got no dreams
- I've got nothing!

Can I make a bold statement? (If you answered "no", then you had best go to the next heading and read on, otherwise brace yourself.) *You have got nothing, unless you have got Jesus Christ in your life.* You might have nice friends, a nice car and a nice pay packet, but unless you have the hope of Jesus Christ within your heart and you are living for eternity, you have got nothing. The Bible says,

> *"Do not store up for yourselves treasures on earth, where moth and rust destroy, and where thieves break in and steal. But store up for yourselves treasures in heaven..."*   (Matthew 6:19–20)

The truth that changes the facts

There is a truth that underlies the story in John 21. In verse one it says that Jesus was standing by the sea of Tiberius. This was also known as Lake Gennesaret or the Sea of Galilee. The word "Gennesaret" literally means "princely garden, adjoining the fertile plains of Capernaum". (I'll try not to get too technical at this point. Stay focused because I want to make a simple truth.)

In other words, Jesus is standing on "fertile land"! He's standing in a place of provision and a place of plenty. He calls out to the disciples (and you too) and He says, "Have you caught anything? Have you found what you're looking for?" Jesus has got "more than enough". The Bible says,

- God owns the cattle on a thousand hills (Psalm 50:10)
- He has more than enough for you (Ephesians 3:20)

- God has floodgates of blessing and at any moment He can open them up and shower so much blessing upon your life that you won't be able to handle it (Malachi 3:10).

The truth is, Jesus has more than enough! Whatever situation you face or turmoil you are in, God can help you through it. If there's an obstacle, He can help you to overcome it. If you have questions, God has an answer. He's saying, "What can I do?" Jesus is saying to everyone as an individual, "What can I do for you?" Things might be difficult or get difficult, but Jesus can help you. It's incredible. The truth is, He can help! (Try **B.U.R.P.** again – see Face-lift #2)

Finishing the face-lift!

So what fact is there in your life that Jesus cannot change? What need do you have that Jesus cannot deal with?

- THE FACTS are what you are currently experiencing!
- THE TRUTH is there is something more you can experience!

There is a major difference between visiting and knowing truth and actually living in it. It is time for you to live in the truth of what Jesus can do and NOT the facts of what you are currently experiencing. Let me illustrate it this way:

Fact 1: You may be sick
Truth 1: *"By His stripes we are healed"* (Isaiah 53:5) [4]

- The facts are clear (you are sick) and the truth is undisputed (God heals). So what do you do? Remain sick (fact) or believe for the truth of what God can do to be applied to your life?
- You have to apply TRUTH to your FACTS. Pray for healing and talk about God healing you; and continue to believe that God will heal you.
- In other words, you are closing the distance between truth and fact until fact and truth are the same. In this instance, you are healed!

Fact 2: You may worry about everything
Truth 2: *"Therefore I tell you, do not worry about your life"* (Matthew 6:33)

- The fact and truth are both clear.
- Continually remind yourself that although you worry (fact), God is more than able to provide for you and help you through anything and everything (Matthew 6:33; Ephesians 3:20).
- Apply TRUTH (God is in control) to FACT (I am a worrier) and remind yourself of the truth until you close the gap between fact and truth and now you do not worry.

Coming up:
"Losing Georgia"

Notes

1. 'Razz' = drinking too much alcohol.
2. I made up the company name (with help). But it works, don't you think?
3. "Pete Tong" is rhyming slang for "wrong". In Britain, people often speak with rhyming slang, which uses a conjunction of words in which the last word is used to suggest a rhyme that is its definition. For instance, if you say "apple and pears", it means "stairs". "Pete Tong" is also a famous radio DJ for Radio 1 in the UK.
4. There are many verses in the Bible that speak of God wanting to heal us. See James 5:14–15 and 1 Peter 2:24 as examples.

Making it real for you!

1. What do the following terms mean?

   FACT: ....

   ....

   ....

   TRUTH: ....

   ....

   ....

2. List three FACTS that need changing in your life

   (a) ....

   (b) ....

   (c) ....

3. Which three Bible verses teach truths that are opposite to your facts?

   (a) ....

   (b) ....

   (c) ....

4. How can you apply truth to each of your facts?

   (a) ....

   (b) ....

   (c) ....

Someone once said,

"Eagles may soar,
but chickens don't get sucked
into jet engines."

Face-lift #7

If I had a face like yours, I would...

...climb a tree

Although every human on the planet is individual in every way, we also have many things in common. We all have a heartbeat, blood, hair (some of us), life (again – questionable), a desire to be loved and a need to belong. One of the overriding factors that we have in common is that we are all looking for change. We are all looking for something different. My wife used to love watching a TV show called, *Extreme Makeover: Home Edition*. If you haven't seen it, the producers of the show find a family who endure impossible hardships and decide to do something special for them. They send them to Disneyland (or some other location) for a week and in that time, they knock down the family's old house and build them a new incredible home in its place.

All the neighbours give a huge welcome when the family arrive home. They are unable to see the new house because a huge bus is blocking their view, so they all shout, "Hey, bus driver – move that bus!" – and he does! The new house is always stunning – a mansion with luxuries that they could only have dreamed of. I have never seen the families cry because they wanted their old shack back. They always hug each other and run to see their new home. They welcome the change with open arms.

The other day I was watching the news. (Don't be alarmed, it's only because *The Simpson's* wasn't on at the time.) The news reported that some men who represented a certain cause, stormed on to the set of the National Lottery and caused a disruption on live television. The men who ran on to the TV set wanted change for the social issue they believed in and the millions of people watching the Live Lottery Draw were also watching, hoping their numbers would come up so they too could have a change!

We all long for something new. We all want something different to happen to us in life. That is why birthdays are such a big deal. We are not only looking for new presents, but also a new experience to embrace for our lives. For one of my wife's birthdays, I bought her a tandem skydiving experience. She jumped from 12,000ft from a perfectly healthy aircraft. It was not crashing, the engines hadn't failed, nor was she attempting to escape the food on board the plane. It was a planned jump, for people who like risking their lives for fun! She free-fell 5,000ft, which only took forty seconds and then (after much prayer from me and the kids watching from the ground), the parachute opened and it took about six minutes for her to float to the ground! It is something different, it's new and exciting!

In Luke 19:1–10 we read the awesome story of Zacchaeus (Zach) the tax collector. Why not read the story and collect your own thoughts from it! It is on page 927 in my Bible!

Three things Zach did to get a changed life

These three things will also help you to live life differently and give you a face-lift!

1. He acted on God-intrigue

Zach had heard about Jesus and that He was coming to town. He heard enough about Jesus to be intrigued.

- What did Jesus look like?
- What did He sound like?
- Perhaps I can get an autograph.
- I wonder if He is wearing this year's "three-strap style sandal" or last season's "two-strap style"?
- Perhaps He will do that wine miracle thing again and I will get a free drink!

All of that is conjecture – we are not sure what it was about Jesus that intrigued him, but he had heard enough to seek Him out.

There come moments in all our lives when "God-intrigue" kicks in. Moments when we get interested in God and truth. Different events in our life stir up God-intrigue. When 9–11 sparked a wave of neo-terrorism I received a lot of phone calls from people who, for the first time in a long time, had begun to think about God, eternity and truth. Birth, death, age, sickness and having everything money can buy, but still feeling empty, all stir up God-intrigue.

Perhaps as you read these words, something about God is connecting with you and you are beginning to get intrigued, either for the first time or about stuff from long ago. Zach acted on his intrigue. When you act on God-intrigue you are one step closer to living a changed life.

2. He rose above his obstacles

The second thing Zach did to get a changed life was: he rose above his obstacles (literally). In Luke 19:4 it says that Zach, *"climbed a sycamore-fig tree"*. Zach was not the most popular man in the city. In fact, he was one of the most despised men around. He was a tax collector. They were known to be men who cheated people out of money so they could live a more prosperous lifestyle. They made the poor poorer and charged extortionate rates to the middle and upper classes. On the day Zach met Jesus he braved the crowds of people ignoring their mutterings (v. 7) and then, on discovering he could not see, he climbed a tree and literally rose above his obstacles.

Your perspective is completely altered by the elevation you have. This is a great truth for us as we seek to live "changed lives".

When my daughter was three, I lost her in a department store. One minute she was holding my hand and the next second she was gone. After calling her name calmly for ten seconds with no response, I ran to the exit of the store and asked them to shut the doors. When the doors were closed, the staff and I ran around trying to find her. I was panicking! The problem was that I could not see over the racks of clothes – she could have been anywhere. So I rode the escalator up to the second floor. On the way up, I could see over the racks of clothes, so I had a great bird's eye view of the shop. My elevation completely changed my perspective. The racks of clothes that were previously obstacles to me, were now nothing. Then I saw Georgia, sucking her thumb near the check-outs. Phew! I nearly hugged her to death.

In Ephesians 1:20 it says that Jesus sits in *"heavenly places"*. His elevated view gives Him a great perspective on our lives. Ephesians 2:6 goes on to say that, *"God **raised us up** with Christ and seated us with him in the heavenly realms in Christ Jesus"* (emphasis added). Relationship with Christ means that your elevated position gives you a different perspective. Where previously obstacles seemed insurmountable, now you begin to get God's perspective. You can now see past the obstacles as, *"all things are possible"* (Matthew 19:26).

In life you can get a better education, read self-help books or even climb a tree. But only God can give you a permanent change of perspective on life.

3. He changed his mind

The third thing Zach did to change his life was: he changed his mind. In verse 8 Zach said that he was going to give away half of his possessions to the poor and give back to those he had cheated four times the amount he took! His change of mind preceded a change of life. His change of mind preceded a change of action.

In Romans 12:2 it says, *"Be transformed by the renewal of your mind"*! The mind is the place where you formulate **how** you do things.

Repentance means changing the way you do things. "To

repent" does not just mean to say sorry, it means to turn around, to change – to live differently! That is exactly what Zach did in verse 8.

Perhaps you need to change your mind today? Why not change your mind and change your actions. This is step number three in living the different life you know you need to live. Ask God to help you to live out these new actions.

Three things Jesus did to change Zach's life

1. Jesus was prepared to be interrupted

In Luke 19:1 it says that Jesus was *"passing through"* Jericho. He was on His way to somewhere. He hadn't intended to stay in Jericho. He was busy ... but not too busy for Zach.

Amazingly, the majority of the miracles that Jesus accomplished in His three years of ministry took place while He was on His way somewhere else. He would travel to a place, but on the journey, stop and do great things for people He met along the way.

I once used to have a neighbour whose nickname was "Sorry Man"! I don't know the intimate details of his upbringing, but every conversation with him proved to be infuriating. It seemed like he said "sorry" several times in every single sentence. On one classic occasion there was a knock at the door ... yep, it was "Sorry Man". The conversation between "Sorry Man" (SM) and me (M) went as follows:

> [SM]: "I'm sorry!"
> [M]: "That's Ok. What's up?"
> [SM]: "I'm sorry!"
> [M]: "That's Ok! What's up?"
> [SM]: "I am sorry to tell you that ... I'm sorry ... but, I am sorry that ... "
> [M]: (sigh)
> [SM]: "I was looking out of the window, sorry ... "
> [M]: "That's Ok, that's what windows are for!"
> [SM]: "Yeah, but I am sorry ... I saw something ... sorry!"
> [M]: "That's Ok. What did you see?"
> [SM]: "Sorry!"
> [M]: "It's truly Ok. What did you see?"
> [SM]: "Sorry to tell you that I saw ... I'm sorry!"
> [M]: (wanting to die) "What did you see?"
> [SM]: "I am sorry, but I saw a rat in the garden!"
> [M]: "Oh!" (What do you say to that? "OH, MY GOODNESS, NOT A RAT!")
> [SM]: "I'm sorry."
> [M]: "That's Ok!" (Why is he saying sorry? Did he put it there?)

Now it's confession time. There were times that I needed to go out, but on the way I would see "Sorry Man" washing his car and think to myself, "If I go out there I am in for another LONG, POINTLESS DISCUSSION involving a lot of sorrys!" So, I would hide until the coast was clear. Other times I would come home and see "Sorry Man" outside the front of his house. I would drive around the block until the coast was clear. Sometimes I did it because I was tired and couldn't handle a whole bunch of sorrys, but mostly I did it because I was too busy!

Jesus, on the other hand is always happy to be interrupted. The reason Jesus does this in the story of Zach is because God's nature is that He is prepared to change His schedule according to your needs. Jesus had not planned to stay in Jericho that day. He was just *"passing through"*. However, something about Zach (perhaps his desire to see Jesus) caused Jesus to stop and say, "Come down immediately. Today I must stay at your house!" Wow, God changed His plans for a little man!

Wherever you are in life, you have to understand that God is not too busy for you. There are six billion people on the planet and God is interested in **you.** You are not just a face in the crowd. You are not just a number in heaven's roll of honour. You are someone who God is passionately committed to. The Bible says that "God knows all about a sparrow's life – but you are worth far more to Him" (see Luke 12:7). The point is quite simple, if God has the capacity to know about the life-cycle of a bird, He is more than capable of having enough time for you. In fact the term *el-Shaddai*[1] means "more than enough". God is not too busy. Why not have a talk with Him for a while today; you will find that He is more than ready to listen AND talk back (B.U.R.P.).

2. Jesus threw His lot in with Zach

The second thing Jesus did to change Zach's life was: He threw His lot in with Zach! In verse 5 Jesus says, *"I must come to your house today*!" Zach was a man despised above most others. Jesus didn't mind what "other" people thought about Zach. Jesus wasn't someone who associated with people because it made Him look good. Jesus wasn't so concerned with how He looked, He just wanted to make sure that Zach looked good and felt fulfilled in everything! Today, Jesus would associate with anyone who wants a changed life!

Zach didn't have the ability to change his life on his own. No amount of self-help books could help him enough to change his life substantially for eternity. The only way he could truly have his life changed was to connect with Jesus; to let Jesus spend time with him, change his mind on his lifestyle and act accordingly.

The best thing you can do for a changed life is "let Jesus" throw His lot in with you. You can change certain areas of your life without Jesus' help, but for a truly life-changing experience that lasts into eternity, Jesus is your best bet.

3. Jesus acknowledged Zach's decision

The last thing Jesus did to bring change to Zach's life was: He acknowledged Zach's decision. In Luke 19:9 Jesus says, *"Today salvation has come to this house"*! Jesus made a point of not delaying in acknowledging Zach's change of heart! Jesus did not say, "Are you sure Zach?" or "Zach, this decision does not affect your statutory rights," or "Would you like to take up the money-back guarantee offer?" or "Would you like forty days to think it over so you don't make an emotional decision?"

Jesus takes up Zach on his offer immediately! Right now where you are, Jesus is prepared to listen to you and take you at face value on the things you say.

Finishing the face-lift!

Today would be a great day to make some life-changing decisions. You could decide...

- To quit some addictive behaviour
- To stop a cycle of thinking
- To repent from your way of life
- To attend a Bible or leadership training college
- To get more involved in church life
- To pray and read your Bible more (**B.U.R.P.**)
- To pursue the call of God on your life without delay

Whatever your decision, give it to God in prayer today, act on what you say and watch God help you to change your life!

The name Zacchaeus means "pure". He was anything but pure. He was unethical and immoral. However, when he connected with Jesus, he became everything he was meant to be. When you connect with Jesus, He helps you to become everything you were meant to be too, but you've got to want to change!

Coming up:
"The End!"

Note

1. A Hebrew name for God found throughout Genesis and Exodus.

Making it real for you!

1. Which areas of your life would you like to change?

   ....

   ....

   ....

2. Which obstacles hold you back from pursuing a different lifestyle from how you currently live and how can you rise above them?

   ....

   ....

   ....

3. Which three Bible verses teach truth that is opposite to your facts?

   (a) ....

   (b) ....

   (c) ....

4. What habits do you need to deal with once and for all?

   ....

   ....

   ....

5. Ask God to help you to rise above the obstacles, deal with habits and live changed.

Someone once said,

"The easiest way to find
something lost around the house
is to buy a replacement."

The last bit!

A little boy was sitting in church with his granddad. He saw a list of names on the wall near to where he was sitting and so he whispered, "Granddad, who are those people on the wall over there?" Granddad replied, "They are the names of men and woman who have died in the services over the years." The little boy thought about it for a while and then said, "Granddad, did they die in the morning service or the evening service?"

So what do you think? Have you had a face-lift? My prayer for you is that everything about the way you do Christianity changes from this point on because you have...

- Remembered that KFC sells chicken (it's all about Jesus)
- Remembered that living for Jesus is flippin' brilliant!
- Decided to be a spaceship! (Thrown off the labels people have pinned on you.)
- Chosen enthusiasm!
- Decided to "Go, then leave!" (Leave the past behind.)
- Ignored the facts!
- Climbed a tree!

With such a face-lift I think that you will hear people begin to say to you, *"I don't know what you are smoking, drinking, chewing or injecting, but I gotta get me some of that!"*

I believe in you! You are awesome!

Coming up
"If I knew what happened next!"

Someone once said,

"Whenever I feel blue,
I start breathing again!"